The Soul's Journey II:
Emotional Archaeology

Tom Jacobs

By Tom Jacobs

Books
Living Myth: Exploring Archetypal Journeys
Seeing Through Spiritual Eyes: A Memoir of Intuitive Awakening
The Soul's Journey I: Astrology, Reincarnation, and Karma with a Medium and Channel
Saturn Returns: Thinking Astrologically
Chiron, 2012, and the Aquarian Age: The Key and How to Use It
Lilith: Healing the Wild

Channeled Material
Approaching Love
Understanding Loss and Death
Goddess Past, Present, and Future
Conscious Revolution: Tools for 2012 and Beyond
Djehuty Speaks

Natal Reports
The True Black Moon Lilith Natal Report
Living in the Present Tense Natal Report/2012 Prep Course

ISBN-13: 978-1452805665
ISBN-10: 1452805660

Acknowledgements

Heartfelt thanks go to each of the participants in the Emotional Archaeology workshop for their openness in sharing their life stories. The principles behind the workshop amount to very little if individuals are not open to seeing their lives and learning to see themselves in new ways, and this workshop was a wonderful experience for me as a teacher as a result of their openness.

Extra special thanks go to Candace Meils for producing and hosting the weekend workshop.

Introduction: Making Peace With How We Got Here

Some of my earliest memories in this life are of being curious about why people do what they do. I was intrigued with watching people do mundane tasks of all kinds but the scale went all the way up observing how a person's life unfolded. The psychology behind choices was fascinating to this Scorpio as a little one. After I found out that we are energetic beings with all that implies regarding our relationship with emotion and memory –and how emotion and memory inform belief and therefore choice – my observations of individual humans on small and large scales took on new importance. It didn't happen overnight but now it's my profession to observe people and help them see themselves in new light, as energetic beings with all that implies.

These days I often find myself in wonderment at the life process we each go through. This human thing we're each doing presents challenges and enticements to grow and we each respond in unique ways and at our own rates of speed to particular sets of stimuli presented. Each of us has free will to make choices that work best for us but it's also true that each of us carries multilife memories and associated beliefs about why things happen. *These memories and beliefs determine what we allow to be possible and very directly determine the choices that we make.* My approach to evolutionary astrology has become rooted firmly in this conception of how a human creates a self based on the multilife journey and its related experiences, and my work in all its forms seeks to share this perspective.

I taught the workshop titled Emotional Archaeology over the weekend of September 10-11, 2011 in Yakima, Washington to a group of 7. A client of mine living there had built a yurt on her property in order to host and facilitate events such as this one and the timing was such that this workshop was the first hosted there. There was an intimacy about the proceedings as most of the workshop participants had known each other for years. The informal, friendly tone of friends and even family members (Candace and Summer are sisters) makes its way into the transcription as I felt it important to retain the quality of connectedness that a number of us felt doing this work together. Additionally, I had done work with 3 of the 7 participants as clients prior the workshop and 4 of us are members of Evolutionary Astrologer Steven Forrest's Apprenticeship Program, so there were shared experiences and vocabulary among some of us on those levels, too.

Listening to the life stories of the participants while working with their astrological birth charts during the workshop was a special experience for me for a few

6

reasons. In large part this was because I had the opportunity to help each one in turn change their minds about the course their lives had taken to that point. Many of us can sooner or later and in some way figure out how to find peace where we are but it can be another thing entirely to make peace with how we got here. Adding insights about the nature and path of soul to the soul-level intentions and wounding we each carry – the normal purview of this niche approach we call evolutionary astrology – can put us on a fast-track to embodying peace about the often convoluted paths on which our life journeys have taken us. The workshop was intended not only to teach the principles of my version of evolutionary astrology but also to put words to many experiences that the participants had in life that might not have been understood in terms of their multilife karmic journeys.

At the end of the process of transcribing the workshop for the present volume, I am even more deeply settled into that state of wonder about the human experience. A particular moment inspired me to begin writing this introduction. It was when I reheard Summer reflect on what she has learned in this life after radical path alterations that challenged her at different points along the way. But it's not just her story alone that inspires me – each of the participants reflects lessons learned that are in fact indicative of karmic healing. If I ever need inspiration to continue counseling clients, writing, and teaching about soul and evolutionary astrology, all I need to do is to talk to a human about what he or she has observed and learned about the self so far. People are amazing and if we're paying attention and open to changing, maybe we don't need evolutionary or any other kind of astrology. It helps in many ways but humans are clever and resourceful. A bit of attention and awareness is all that's really needed to be in a state of healing the karmic past and understanding more about who we are.

My intention for this book is that it offer a unique glimpse into the human experience so that you can begin to transform your relationship with life, the Universe, yourself, and everyone else who populates your sphere. Sound like a tall order for a little old book, right? But given the perspectives on evolutionary astrology presented here and the impact I see them have on people all the time, I don't think it is. They were first in print in *The Soul's Journey I: Astrology, Reincarnation, and Karma with a Medium and Channel* and are expanded upon here in depth. They open doors into understanding all facets of our life experience. Instead of arriving at the point at which we refeel that pain from another life and begin to traffic in vocabulary reflecting that we feel the way we do, with the information in these two books we can go several steps further and learn to relate to our souls as real entities with a definite, Divine plan. We can then see that our lives to date have reflected the Divine intentions of the soul. The birth chart reflects that plan and learning to read it in this way enables us to bring its wisdom into our lives. This not only helps guide our choices going forward to serve us better on all levels but also helps put the past into proper perspective: *we can make peace with how we got here, wherever that happens to be.*

What results can shift our experience of ourselves and of life itself and I argue that there is no more empowering exercise for a human. We can suddenly gain a new lease on life and/or an influx of optimism or faith by seeing things in a different light. Life isn't solely about happiness and fulfillment but each of us has the right and opportunity to create them for ourselves and, often, understanding and unraveling the past and our attachment to it is the key to doing so.

As mentioned above, the first volume in this series contains the core principles of this work with soul and astrology and the 4-step method of chart analysis I use and on which the Emotional Archaeology workshop was based. The material here expands upon the principles and method of analysis as it brings in the reflections and first-person stories of people living the charts out in the real world. Each of the individual stories contained here reflects that the chart holder has learned an important lesson in this life indicated in the chart as a vexing influence across many lives. This is wonderful, to be sure, but in fact necessary to real understanding: we can't know how a person lives the chart until we interact with him or her. If we use these or other astrological principles in a vacuum – without listening to the person the chart belongs to – we run the risk of getting academic and, perhaps, less than helpful to the real, live person in front of us. For this reason I feel this book is an important tool to support teaching the unique brand of evolutionary astrology I practice. The material has become the second volume in *The Soul's Journey* series because understanding the depth of chart analysis and emotion that goes with this material is the next step in the longer *The Soul's Journey* story that has formed in my mind.

The Pluto Generations section that appears after the 4-step Method of Chart Analysis section appears in the workshop recording after the 3rd of the 7 example charts. It has been placed before the example charts in the text so that the reader can have that context going into the sections containing the example charts. It was not planned to be part of the weekend but a participant who understands how fundamental that information is to how I think about Pluto – and that Pluto is in fact central to how I do astrology – asked me to explain it in detail and it made sense to do so.

Regarding the text, it is a transcription. I have edited it but attempted to remain true to the original spirit of what was said. Much of the casual, conversation tone has been left in including colloquialisms and slang.

Enjoy the material and feel free to take apart your own chart and all others in your possession to see how you really tick and why.

Tom Jacobs
Tucson, AZ
October 24th, 2012

Emotional Archaeology

Our focus in these two days is on what I call emotional archaeology. We can think about the imagery of regular archaeology: finding a piece of land, isolating a piece of land that might have goodies buried in it. Then methodically uncovering the strata of Earth, the layers, and intentionally focusing on gently looking at what's there, getting out our little brushes and dusting off the dust around things, but to catalog these layers going down – doing that with emotions.

I have done this with every client I've worked with for years and Candace and I were talking about the idea of me coming back here.[1] In that conversation I was explaining this idea of emotional archaeology and how I do it with birth charts and she said, "I want to learn that!" I said, "Gosh, I've never taught that to anybody, I just use that with and on people. I just use it in my work." Sometimes people ask in the middle of the process, "Well, what are you doing?" And I will explain for a moment but at those

---

[1] In July of 2011 I toured the Northwest doing channeling events and Candace hosted a handful of them in the yurt.

times we are in the process. Candace and I agreed that this workshop would be to teach you how to do this but also use your charts so that you can really get inside the process as I do it with you, as we talk about it from the bird's-eye view. This does include evolutionary astrology, which is a way of looking at us as multidimensional beings – so we are going to talk about reincarnation and the soul, and why your soul has chosen to wire you as a human the way that it has. When we talk about soul we are going to talk about you as the Divine creator who has split off to forget it for a while – to forget that you are a Divine creator.

So that you think you are Michael. You are living your life and you will have an idea of the spiritual eventually at some point in your multilife journey, but to actually reconnect with the truth that you have created all that you've experienced, which takes us closer to soul. Part of this is looking at a birth chart as reflecting the soul's intentions.

The intention is always to be gentle when we find something in the dirt and brush away the debris around it. One of my core intentions is to support people in discovering and uncovering this past that each person carries in order to be able to let go of some of it so that we can become present in our living. That's the whole goal of this. My definition of "spiritual" includes presence. What does it mean to be spiritual? It doesn't have anything to do with the tools, or the books, or the people who offer training in what we think of as spiritual. It doesn't have anything to do with how many meditations I give you. It's your experience of becoming present, of coming out of identifying with the strata of emotional history that you're carrying.

So that's my goal here. And we're going to take different routes that might seem all the way around the block and then like over to Ellensburg and back, but it's all about getting you present and supporting you in coming to be more present.

Looking at these emotions we carry deep down, having the intention to connect more with soul, understanding the intentions of soul, and then aligning with the fact that we have created it – becoming closer to soul in this way raises your consciousness. It shifts your awareness. One of the goals here is to give you some tools and insights so that you can look at anything in your life that has happened to you and, with compassion and grace, accept it as your creation as God and Goddess. This takes us a little beyond regular evolutionary astrology, which is already beyond regular astrology. My experiences working as a psychic medium with the spirits of those who have passed away have taught me about how they perceive everything once they pass. This is both in how their human personalities might be – they might not want to give up yet things they were attached to as people, and I can see that, and then also when they do release it they gain a bird's-eye view on why their life was the way it was including why all of their relationships happened. I have experienced their wonderment, joy, confusion, and the light bulbs going off about why they created what they created. That's been an incredible experience, to work with people who are on their way out of being attached to being human and they're getting the education about what their soul created.

My experiences as a channel have involved a lot of direct questions about soul to the Ascended Master I work with.[2] People ask me how I got involved in channeling and I think one of you asked me that yesterday. I've mentioned in different places the story about how I had some questions I wasn't getting answered in books or from human astrologers about soul. I realized that lots of Eastern traditions and spiritual traditions will focus on it but something was lacking – something was missing for me, wasn't resonating with me. This Ascended Master came forward and started answering the questions I was holding in my mind. So from the Ascended Master I learned about why a soul picks the lives it picks and why the birth chart is the way it is: *Why* is Pluto in Cancer? *Why* is the South Node in the 6th house? Not just trying to understand the fact of what it means that it's there – how it plays out in your day-to-day life – but *why*.

I'm a very curious person and I seem to be willing to do a tremendous amount to satisfy that curiosity [laughs]. I seem to be willing to –

Candace: Far-reaching – faaaar reaching…

Tom: Right? I can't stop.

Candace: Yay! Thank you. Thank you so much. [several laugh]

---

[2] Ascended Master Djehuty, a.k.a. Thoth, St. Germain, and Merlin.

Tom: It's a Scorpio thing: whatever you see in front of you, you say, "why?" And then you get an answer and you see that answer and you're like, "Well, that's great, but *why*?" For the first time in my life I found the point at which I didn't have to keep asking "why" because I had it revealed to me, and that's why we're here.

We're going to talk about, for each of you, *why*. Not just, "can you get over it?" Or, "what could you do to feel better about it?" Or, "can you forgive somebody or yourself for a choice?" But *why* your soul has created it. For me, that's what's been missing from astrology.

Candace: Yes.

Tom: Oh yes, for you, too. You resonate so strongly with this.

Candace: Yeah.

Tom: I still call it evolutionary astrology but sometimes I call it evolutionary astrology plus – to spend an hour talking about what soul is – that's new. That's new.

Backtracking to our talk last night,[3] and I think everyone here was here, we are energetic beings. And then backtracking to perhaps before the beginning of that, All That Is or the great Divine Intelligence – which is *everything*, all consciousness – realized that it couldn't know itself when a whole. The decision was made to partition itself off with the intention of temporarily forgetting its true nature as All That Is or the Divine Intelligence. Not just to temporarily forget but to also be

---

[3] "Chiron and Human Evolution."

embodied. And that's what you are – that's what we are, and that's what Bodhi and Goodman[4] are, and that's what our bird friends are: portions of this Divine Intelligence – and yes, even bugs and cockroaches. [laughs] After I tell this whole thing I sometimes get asked, "Well, what about bugs and cockroaches?" And, "Should I not kill mosquitoes?" And, "Am I killing God?" But I struggle with that, too, finding the consciousness within that being.

And so the intention is to temporarily forget so that we can eventually remember while embodied. But the in-between time – which is vast, which is millions of years – is experiential learning while being ignorant of what's happening. [group laughs]

Tom: The vast, vast, vast time between during which Divine Source says, "Aha, I'm going to partition myself off and embody, temporarily forgetting my true nature and then eventually remembering" leaves out the millions-of-years montage of experiential learning through ignorance. Where you are now that makes you want to come here and hang out with us, where you are now and where humans have the opportunity to be given the evolution of consciousness that the Mayan Calendar tracks,[5] is drawing a line in the sand in your history, in your experience as a being. Everything that you have encountered to-date

---

[4] Candace's dog and cat, respectively.
[5] Much of the "Chiron and Human Evolution" talk the night before was based on teachings about the Mayan Long Count Calendar having been designed as a metric to track the stages of the evolution of consciousness.

according to the Earth time line – for thousands and millions of years – everything that your portion of the Divine Intelligence has experienced has more or less been through ignorance – great. Draw a line in the sand and say, "Okay, I accept that." Emotional Archaeology is about processing the results of the experience that has been gained through ignorance, which has been more or less half painful. Or roughly half of the experiences have been painful, to say it another way. This vast duration of time allows for this incredible array of experiences which have all been brought through ignorance.

For a few decades a lot of us have been getting exposed to these ideas that we can create our reality and that's great, but it's not enough. We also have to understand why we created it, even though through ignorance. As we talk today and tomorrow about all these things, I'm going to ask that you plant a seed – and that you return to drizzle some water on it occasionally, whenever you remember – and it is to forgive yourself for having created through ignorance what has been painful. Each of us does have an inner judge that might want to come forward and say, "Really? I created that? Ach..." And we just want to release ourselves. Part of this drawing a line in the sand is also letting that judge just be wired the way it is but not feed it. The intention of you as Divine Source is to have created through ignorance – and you've done it. That was the intention.

It's amazing to me that we're only just now capable of using a birth chart like this. Think about the threads of

17

understanding that you have gathered in your life, that you've woven together into philosophies and teachings, lifestyles, and practices – the things that you're already pretty savvy about spiritually and metaphysically – but now because of this ramping up of the evolution of consciousness now we're able to do more with it. It's almost like we've been gathering these threads in our pockets and weaving them together, but now we can actually see how to put them all together to make a rope to use to climb out of the tower – whatever.

Glenna: It's more accessible. I see a picture of building, a grocery store, but there's no entrance really.

Tom: Great! Yes. Thank you.

Candace: Drawbridge.

Tom: Right. Why do you say "grocery store?"

Glenna: I saw this grocery store with no entrance but now there's this big door – here we go with the goodies.

Tom: Learning the "why" is akin to that – seeing the door and being able to figure things out finally.

The other thing about being a human that you probably all noticed is the inborn need we have to find or create meaning. The why sates that – the answer to why you've created your journey how you have sates it.

I was on this search for meaning and just in the last few years I was able to start to chill out. [laughs] After thousands of years of trying to figure out what was really going on.

To talk about the multilife journey of this Divine Intelligence, I've had the image of a soul sitting with its advisory team – its guidance team – in some sort of conference-room type situation. On the wall is a huge array of monitors. The meeting begins with the soul being asked by the guidance team, "What do you wanna do? What are you gonna learn about as you forget your nature and stumble through blind ignorance for thousands of lifetimes to learn what it means to do so?" The soul says, "Um, I'm gonna learn about equality, justice, and fairness." And the guidance team says, "Oh, that's a good one, that's a really good one! Yeah, that sounds good." And so the soul, outside time, then basically erupts into space-time but the soul is outside space-time. Your life is one of these eruptions. Each life is like a tendril into this dimension.

What you experience is fed back to the soul. I get this image of the monitors on the wall. Your life is one of these thousands of monitors associated with this soul. With the theme of justice, fairness, and equality – which is Libra/7th house/Venus, by the way – all of these different lives give the soul the opportunity to learn about different choices in different social, family, and economic contexts.

All these lives are eruptions into this dimension including your life. You're going about your business. You're like, "Well, this is what I want to study in school. I want to have a family. I want to live here. I want to have this kind of life." We think that's what's really happening – we're not connected to soul at all – and that's the sickness of the world that we have been living, I believe.

Michael: Like a separation from soul.

Tom: Yes, exactly. You're separated from Divinity because you don't understand who you are and you're separated from each other but you don't understand that everybody else is Divine, that we are together the Divine. Exactly – the perception of separation, with the feeling and the heartache of separation. We need meaning – we need to know there's a purpose. We need to know what we are, right? My quick way to do that is get people connected to soul. There are many routes to spiritual development but that's what I do.

Reconnecting to soul in a more conscious way, which is what we're here to do, and teach you how to help other people do the same thing …

Anne: Can you talk about what you believe about when a person, the soul, has this discussion with the group, but is not aware that it is Divine?

Tom: The soul is aware.

Anne: The soul is, but when he makes a choice, he is not in touch with the soul.

Tom: Using the image of the conference room outside space-time, the soul is sitting in this room. All of its lives are not aware. It erupts into the space-time dimension in order to make choices and experience making choices, but those that are individual humans as opposed to the soul that is associated with me – but yeah, Tom Jacobs has no idea. For the vast majority of Earth history, he and other individuals have no idea. He's thinking, "I love this computer. I'm a writer. I like macaroni" and that kind of thing. "You're cute and you're nice, and I don't like that" and that's what we are occupied with. [group laughs] But the soul is sitting in this room observing the choices. I'm obsessed with the theme of fairness or justice though as a human I might not understand why. I will see the world in terms of it being fair or not fair but the soul is very clear, very aware. The soul is saying, "Well, Tom Jacobs makes this choice to do this within relationship as he seeks fairness – how to create it – but he kind of makes some bonehead moves once in a while." It says, "Ah yes, that outcome is what happens when a human, conditioned and wired as Tom Jacobs is in his time-space context, family context, and karma" – all that stuff – "makes the choice to not reveal the truth to his friend." Let's use that as an example. The soul says, "Aha, when he chooses not to reveal the truth to his friend when it's really important for him to do so, here's what he feels later and that's how it affects the friend, and here's how their relationship might hit a fork in the road because of that." The soul is saying, "Wonderful! I am learning through Tom Jacobs about this choice." Tom Jacobs is feeling pain. The soul is observing the results of choices. Does that make sense?

Group: Yes.

Tom: So imagine this room with all these monitors. The soul sees over here a Roman housewife – same soul. Over here a slave in Mississippi in 1821. Over there, a priest in 1920s Chicago. All these different lives. The soul is getting, "Well, when I am the priest and I don't reveal the truth and don't have equal relationships, then that's what that feels like in that context. Okay. And then this

Roman housewife, when she doesn't say the thing she needs to say, this is what she experiences." The soul is aware of all of that input.

Now, we are experiencing time and we're on this trajectory from birth to maturation and unfolding to death. But the soul is observing all of these lives simultaneously. It would be like having a TV here with something on it recorded in a different time – that program that's coming to us isn't live. It's recorded in a different time, outside the time that we are living in, though it tracks the same way – 10 seconds are 10 seconds. But it was recorded in a different time and it's coming through to us and that's how the soul experiences this.

The focus for soul is making choices and dealing with the results of choices. When I work with people – and we'll talk about this when we talk about Plutonian empowerment and healing – we look at the fact that we have made all kinds of different choices in these various lives. However we are disposed right now to think about what we might choose or what we feel about what we should do, it is the result of choices over many lives. So if I'm hesitant to tell my friend the truth, it's kind of like I am unconsciously weighing the option, and I don't even know I'm doing it; I'm just feeling the emotions and the effects of what's happening in all of my lives – and this conversation is about seeing the bird's-eye view and be able to manage it consciously. But normally, me, Tom Jacobs, being forthright with a friend, doesn't even realize that his feeling about it right now is shaped by a thousand lives of exploring fairness and friendship. [laughs]

Summer: You can sit back consciously in that memory.

Tom: Exactly.

Summer: In that wholeness. We can tap into that wholeness that we are as souls together. We can bring that into our foundation, grounded in spirit.

Tom: Yes. You've been on a path and are in the minority. Eventually, that's where everyone gets. Maybe with different vocabulary and different language – and different skin colors in different times – but that's where we all ultimately go. We will each of us remember our true nature.

Almost all the work I do with anybody about any topic is for cleaning up that vast stretch of time and number of lives that are filled with learning through ignorance.

Annette: So if I come to you with something that's going on in my life, the feeling is – the emotion is ... when something triggers that deep emotion, just to be that Divine Source helps. Just to be with it. Divine Source doesn't really judge it, it just watches it?

Tom: Right.

Annette: And then at some point there's an "aha!" Realizing this is a memory from a page in my life – "oh, I got that."

Tom: Right.

Annette: So I'm cleaning up my vista, right, more than on just this [life's] level? My karma, my everything?

Tom: Yes.

Annette: Are there many things?

Tom: There are a handful.

Annette: Oh, really? So there's structure to that? Like the ten commandments, if you know what I mean? [group laughs]

Tom: Well, I'm going to stay far away from that. There are a handful of themes. We're talking about 12 astrological archetypes – a handful of themes for each person.

Tom: Right. As I said that this soul over here that's erupted into Jacobsville –

Annette: You're a Scorpio –

Tom: Yes, but all that is Pluto in Libra. The soul says, "I'm going to major in justice, fairness, equality, harmony, balance, relationship."

Annette: So your Scorpio has to get to the depth of it, then.

Tom: Yes, but the Scorpio part of it is really the conscious personality as opposed to the soul's intention, which is Pluto – we'll get there. So there are a handful of themes. As we talk about this we'll talk about themes related to the symbols of your Pluto, we'll talk about themes related to your South Node of the Moon, and the South Node ruler of the Moon, and also the North Node to some degree.

Annette: Part of me goes, "Could it really be that simple?"

Group: [yeses and laughter]

Glenna: Because finally there's a door to get in there.

Tom: We're going to list the themes that each of you is majoring in at the soul level and we're going to rank what this life is focusing on. An example is that I have a past life where I have the dude's chart. My South Node is in Cancer in the 10th house, and my Pluto is in my 12th house. Those indicate two major themes for me of that handful of themes. He has South Node in the 12th house, where my Pluto is in my chart. And I have my South Node where his Pluto is – Cancer in the 10th. So the soul is focusing on varying degrees in different lives – with weights and balances – of certain themes but in some other life I could have Moon conjunct my South Node, which echoes South Node in Cancer.

That guy has South Node in the 12th and I have Pluto in the 12th – we're kind of exchanging thematic emphases. We're varying them but 10th house and 12th house are big for me. We trade in these themes. I also have squares to my nodes, which we'll talk about, but there is a heavy emphasis on Venus stuff for me – needing to learn new things about Venus. Basically being habituated to Venus stuff but needing to learn new things. And so in some other life I might not have Venus and Chiron in Venus's house square the nodes – I might not have that same setup but the emphasis on needing to learn new things about Venus will be there in different ways.

With that example, that guy has Pluto in Cancer in the 10th and my South Node is in Cancer in the 10th. In some other life this soul might manifest – or probably does manifest – with Moon conjunct South Node. So it's like this trading of all these themes. It's not to say that Cancer, Moon, and the 4th house are all the same; it's not to say that there's no difference between these members of the archetype but it is to say that the themes will be present in the chart, and there's going to be a handful of them. Twelve archetypes in infinite variety of combinations, myriad combinations as we talk about this.

Anne: So you have a chart now during this life, obviously. What happens to the fact that we haven't had the same birth chart for all these previous lives?

Tom: Similar themes. Not the same chart but similar themes. For example, talking about the South Node of the Moon, it takes about 18.6 years to make a revolution all the way around the wheel. So that's one cycle. About a year and a half per sign.

Annette: Can you use that illustration in your book about the soul?

Tom: Oh, you like that?

Annette: Yeah. Visually, that really helps.

Tom: Anne, have you seen the visual of this in the book?

Anne: No.

Tom: I'm going to hand it to you right now. [Walks to get book, finds page.]

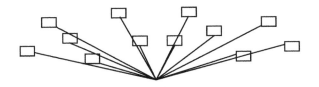

The Soul Is The Source And Has No Beginning Nor End

Figure 1a: The Soul's Relationship To Its Many Lives

Looking at the first one, it's all these lives connected to one point.

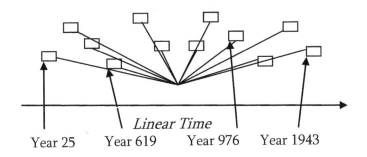

Figure 1b: The Soul's Relationship To Its Many Lives And Linear Time

But then the second one adds the time line and the years. So with these cycles – say it's the nodes of the Moon with the almost 19-year cycle. Well, Pluto represents another theme and that's a 248-year cycle. So if your soul is learning about Cancerian stuff, Pluto's there only every couple hundred years. But the South Node – every 19 years it's there. And then every month, every 28 days, the

Moon's in Cancer. So you have all these different ways of having that theme in a chart. Your souls says, "Roman housewife" over here, and then over there, "trapper-trader." And over here, "camel driver.'" So you're on different places on the time line. In some lives the Cancerian theme is going to be Mars in Cancer square the nodes. In another life it's going to be a South Node in Cancer. In another life it's going to be Pluto in Cancer. You see?

Anne: So even though we had all these lives, our soul is basically still influencing us?

Tom: Oh, yes. All of your experiences in all of these lives are feeding information back to the soul.

Summer: Do you believe that it's the soul that enlivens us?

Tom: Well the soul is sitting in that conference room watching what you're experiencing and learning.

Summer: So a portion of its awareness, or energy comes through?

Tom: Yes. Divine awareness, Divine consciousness, and you are a gathering point – you are collecting data in space-time and the soul is like, "Yes, okay. When Summer does this, this is what happens and this is what it feels like."

Anne: So are you saying that our soul is always guiding us but that we're not aware of it?

Tom: Soul is actually hands-off – sitting back and observing what you're doing. If you want it to guide you, become conscious of what it's about – that's what we're doing today.

Anne: Thank you.

Tom: You're welcome. What happens is that the opportunity becomes to connect to soul, to become consciously with what soul is trying to do. What happens is – and this is what I'm experiencing in my life and am trying to bring to people – you realize all this. You learn about the themes and you can connect with the soul's intentions – why is it creating this, why am I experiencing this? And you kind of feel something with you that has always been there but you've never known how to talk about it or hold space for it. That is the awareness of soul that usually is watching you – you are consciously letting it be here and interact.

That's what you see when you look into the eyes of somebody who's been meditating for years and who has been communing with Spirit in some way. You're seeing the result of that person having opened up to allow soul to come through. So with this idea, "Is it guiding us?" It could. But if I think I'm my shiny sports car or, you know, my physical strength, or my income, I'm naturally just not going to be open to it. But it doesn't actively guide us – and this is important so I'm glad we're going in this direction – it doesn't come in and say, "Well, you should do this and you should not do that." What it does is if you are open to feeling it you will feel resonance: "I should go that way. I should not trust you. I should forgive you." So it can guide us indirectly through resonance.

Michael: Would that be like intuition?

Tom: Yeah, it's part of it, definitely part of it.

Michael: I don't even know why I know that I'm not going to do that. Nothing told me that for sure.

Tom: If you do that on a regular basis and couple that with conscious learning about what the soul is trying to get done – which is what we're doing here – life is magic, life becomes magic. Couple your intuition and gut instinct – it's related – and "what am I really here to do? Why did I get myself born?" Couple those together and bring all that in and life becomes magic. Then you meet the right people at the right time, etc.

Candace: Could you say that one more time? When you couple conscious learning...?

Tom: Oh, yeah: Conscious learning about what the soul is trying to get done *with* that willingness to allow intuition and be connected to inner wisdom.

Michael: Knowingness.

Tom: Knowingness – thank you. Because then the soul just boosts that level of knowingness. I said "magic" but it starts to get surreal, too. You feel like you're 98% in the right place at the right time or you have the opportunity to say, "Oh, I don't want to do that" and this other thing just blossoms, just opens up. Jillian and I were walking in the orchard this morning, eating little fruit things, and she said, "This is a dream." Each of us separately has kind of been more willing to allow that wisdom to come through and to make some choices to support it – being here and doing this workshop is a great thing for each of us. So suddenly we feel this resonance of, "whoa!" It's surreal. Not surreal like I might get nauseous, like I don't know if I can have this conversation with you, but surreal: "*This* is really happening??" That's where there's less resistance for soul to observe and participate – this whole idea of being an open channel.

Glenna: A waking dream.

Tom: Yeah. And as far as this talk about human evolution covered in last night's talk, that's a possibility, to be living in this waking dream. And as far as 2012 and soul goes, it's not that everybody's suddenly happy and everyone gets along and it's the Aquarian Age and we're all like skipping through the fields singing cool songs and eating organic. It's not like some magic thing that happens. It's this: opening up to your multidimensional nature.

Understanding and Changing Karma

So emotional archaeology to dig down is about cleaning up the past and making sure that things are filed appropriately. That's where I want to go next, is karma. So what do we normally think karma is? I want to hear what you have heard, and what you understand, and what you feel, what you sense – what is karma?

Candace: The bad shit. [group laughs]

Tom: Right on. The bad shit.

Candace: That's a concept that's floating around, that it's the bad shit that you brought in.

Tom: Do you remember when – not the moment but the time in your life – when you first heard about karma? How did you hear it? What was going on?

Jillian: That's a good question.

Candace: I had just left the church. I was integrating new teachings. It was the new-age thing about, "Well, you know, you got your karma – you got karma to clean up."

Tom: Okay, great.

Glenna: For me, it was when I was pretty young and I remember I got away with stealing a piece of candy, and I ended up confessing to a friend and they said even if you don't get caught now it's karmic, so ... When I was real little there was that sense of it. The other side of it was more recent with the idea that there is also good karma that catches up with you, that you've done someone a favor in the past. And it was real recent, maybe a year and a half ago, that I started thinking about that.

Tom: Anybody else? When you first heard about karma?

Annette: My first experience was in the church, and speaking to what Candace said, that was the terminology used. But I really feel that we can get off that wheel. I don't believe most of what I hear about it.

Tom: Okay. So I will offer how I understand it and you can take it or leave it. I definitely don't subscribe to it as it's usually talked about. I'm with you on throwing out some of that bathwater first.

Michael: For me it was in Berkeley, about consciousness about expanding, but it was presented as, "We can make a difference by what we do," and "reaping what we sow," so I never got the sense that there was the bad stuff, that we create bad karma. It was that I can make a difference tomorrow by what I do, so it seemed like a pretty positive relationship between me and karma in my first feel for it.

Tom: Great. And then later did you hear that it was all about bad shit? Did you hear that from people elsewhere later?

Michael: I heard that whatever you do you'll probably create a bad result. But I didn't get too involved in that because I thought there were other ways of looking at it. So it was more – what you do; you can make a difference tomorrow – something.

Tom: I like that.

Glenna: This is really funny, Michael, but when you said "reaping what you sow" I wrote "repeating what you sow." [group laughs]

Tom: Well, that's it, huh?!

Group: It's the same thing.

Tom: That's what we end up doing. We sow it once and then we can't stop doing this terrible, stupid thing. [group laughs]

Here's what happens: we have this context of this multilife journey and the soul observing all these things. The fact of the eruption into space-time has an effect on all of the energy fields that you are in your human lives. I talk about your energy field – all of your eruptions into space-time (what we would call past lives but I call our souls' other lives) – each one of those shares an energy field in common. So basically the soul might erupt in 3,200 points along the Earth timeline (a random number). Each one of those shares an energy field.

So you have this essentially unconscious set of mandates, which are the themes the soul has chosen to learn. They are going to happen in each of these lives, one way or another, one form or another, one route or another. The energy fields are all linked. I said you have them in common but maybe it's better to say linked. Let's go back to my example of learning about fairness and equality and being forthright with a friend – being honest when I need to be. In some life I do it and it's empowering. I feel wonderful and the person says, "I'm so glad you said that – thank you for being honest with me about this!" And I note, "Oh, that feels good." So then a part of me unconsciously tracks this and marks that when I am honest, it feels good. Ten years later I remember that and I realize that in some other relationship I'm at the point now at which I was in that other one that I have to say the honest thing. I say it and the person goes, you know, "[String of expletives, name calling], you're terrible, I don't want to be your friend." That hurts and I note, "Oh, if I'm honest, then that hurts." Now, that's one life. But when it happens in 1420s Denmark, you feel it now. This evolution of consciousness has the veils dissolving between dimensions, also the partitions in our consciousness and energy field and therefore the partitions between parts of us that carry feelings in different lives.

That's why the thing that you thought you dealt with 20 years ago is up now. It resonates with and has a similar vibration and pain profile as something major in some other life. So in this life you dealt with for example the sister lying to you, but in some other life the sister energetically stabbing you in the back, lying to you, or betraying you – that was too deep. (Some random sister or the same one as this life.) Now it's like, "I thought I forgave my sister. We've moved on." And you did! But the resonance with this other life is now present because the veil between your portions of consciousness is dissolving.

So I tell my friend the thing that needed to be said in order for our relationship to continue, resolve, or be healthy. And my friend says, "Thank you for telling me" and I note, "When I am honest, it feels good and people like it." That's a belief. It's not true – it's just one thing that happened: I made a choice and there's a response. Ten years later in a different relationship I say the thing and the person goes, "[Anger, disdain, etc.]" and I note the opposite, "Oh, when I'm honest and tell the truth I upset people and it hurts." *That's* a belief, too.

With enough of these beliefs good and bad, belief becomes attached to the emotion in your field. *That's what karma is: the label on a feeling.*

When we become free of karma, we allow all feelings to come and we allow all feelings to then go and we don't attach meaning to them. This line that you've drawn in the sand while saying, "Everything I've created thus far is essentially through ignorance ..."

Glenna: So what is karma?

Tom: Karma is the beliefs attached to emotions, which result from experience.

Michael: Attaching meaning to those.

Tom: Mm-hm. If you lie to me and I make a decision about what it means, then I'll have a knot in my energy field, which is pain, and I will apply an adhesive sticker to it that says, "Men who are the age you are lie." Or "people who wear black shirts can't be trusted." Or, "white people

36

lie." Or, "men are terrible." Or, "life is unfair." "You can't trust anybody, etc." That's what karma is.

Back to the example of me telling a friend something important and being hurt as a result, what happened is that the person did not appreciate my honesty. The person was in a position that day not to receive it – that's what happened. In emotional archaeology, we're going to be digging through all these layers and we're going to find nuggets of belief and then our job is to rewrite the history of why it happened.

Glenna: Here's an important example, because you helped me with this in a session. I was going through a really transformative time and I felt bad that I wasn't vacuuming before my clients came over.

Tom: Oh, I remember that!

Glenna: It makes me laugh every time. You asked me, "Who are you if you don't vacuum?" And I had all kinds of … "lazy slut" … [group laughs]

Tom: She went there fast.

Glenna: And you said, "The fact is, Glenna, that you are a woman who is not vacuuming." [group laughs] "You've chosen not to vacuum." It was very profound for me that all the meaning, all the belief connected with that – the judgment – I was free to float up.

Tom: And we talked about that in terms of your nodal structure, which we'll get into. But having experienced that, now you're getting the back story.

Anne: So in a way you're saying that our beliefs are creating our karma?

Tom: Well, the beliefs are karma. The karma is comprised of beliefs and when we cling to them we recreate the karma. It's like continually pushing a button. You're sitting at a desk and there are all these buttons in front of you on the desk. This one says, "White men lie." [group laughs]

Group: I know!

Tom: So a white guy comes in your office and he sits down and he says, "I'm not going to have that report to you today and here's why," and you're just like ... but the fact is that the guy doesn't have the report done but he's not telling the truth. He's making up an excuse because he's supposed to have it done. And you hit the button: "White men lie." And you're like, "Well, *that's* true." The button is the emotional trigger.

Anne: Is he a mirror of what you were thinking? Is he mirroring you?

Tom: Yes. He's drawn to you because you hold the belief.

Audience: Aha.

Candace: That white men are gonna lie. That white men can lie.

Tom: Yes. That's the truth – white men *can* lie.

Jillian: It can also be that he comes in and he's telling the truth but based on old lies ...

Tom: That's another side of it, too, so even when he is telling the truth you might think, "Well, here's a white guy so I've got my finger on this button, waiting for any sign that you might not be telling the truth." So yes, whether the person's lying or not, thank you.

Whether the person's lying or not, my finger's on that button "white men lie," waiting for any indication. And then it didn't happen so I couldn't hit the button but I still believe it's true. Later my friend takes me to a dinner party. My finger in my mind and heart is still hovering over this button. At this dinner party someone comes in late and says some excuse and I hit it, finally getting to hit that button and have it be true. And the relief because it turned out to be true! You see? We're trying to have the karma be true because we need to have our feelings justified. The feelings from the past – from the other life. We need our feeling justified even if it has nothing to do with this life and no one ever lied to us in this life.

Anne: But in a way, is our energy drawing those people to us who do lie?

Tom: Precisely. So here we are: energetic beings. You are an energetic being with certain contours. You have this knot here labeled "white men lie" and over here is another, "packaged food is a rip off" and over here it's "anyone who says they want to nurture you is cruel" and over here – these knots floating around your field, lodged in it, with these stickers on them, these labels. The fact of the knot broadcasts the label on the knot. So "white men lie" – I'm working on healing past-life Native American stuff, if you can't tell [group laughs] – if I have this I will draw that energy to me because I believe it. So you *are* creating your reality – of course. That teaching is true. And yet we're actually going to go 5 steps beyond that to unravel it but yes, that's true. It came to you because you believed it's true. So if I believe I'm loved, love is going to come to me.

Glenna: So my question in that is is the higher self going to know that you're drawing those things because you want to learn how to unravel it?

Tom: Yeah, you're here to learn about the theme and so the higher self or soul is observing all of this. We want the higher self to police things and help us. Well, the higher self can offer wisdom if consulted but there's no daddy/mommy figure that the soul or higher self becomes. Every individual is the eruption of the Divine into space-time. So you have a guidance team and you know people who know more things about certain topics than you do and you can consult for guidance, and you can find good books and whatever, but you are the prime mover in this experience.

Anne: We're always responsible.

Tom: Always responsible, and again I remind you not to judge, to let the judge take the day off. We are responsible but not so we flagellate ourselves. This unconscious creation is because we're carrying these knots. "I can't be honest with my friend" – there's a knot with a label on it – because I need to learn that, I'm going to draw people who need to learn either the same exact thing or the other side of the coin. If I believe "I can't trust my friend" then the friends I draw are people who feel that nobody trusts them. So it's this ping-pong thing that raises the level of drama. We're passing the mistrust back and forth and it's escalating the level of learning at the soul level as it escalates our stress about it. And then we get to the point when we say, "I can count 18 people in the last 20 years of my life that I couldn't trust," and then we need to go to an evolutionary astrologer. Because then you have a serious pattern and you need to find out what the karma is behind it – what the belief is and why it's there.

There are different categories of karma but not in the sense of the Eastern traditions teaching that you can change this but you can't change that. I am deeply offended by that nonsense. There are things that are more difficult to change because you're not done learning them, but nothing is off the table for change. Just in case I wanted to reference it I brought this text[6] on Jyotish, which commonly though mistakenly Vedic or Indian astrology. It talks about Sankhya philosophy, which is the cosmology of that ancient culture. It lists the kinds of karma that can and can't be changed; it explains all this karma. I just can't buy it because of what I've been shown about what I'm telling you – if I don't trust then I draw people I can't trust.

Annette: The culture's a caste system.

Tom: Yeah, that too – the caste thing kind of comes later. This original thing is what the ancient seers said, "This is who we are and where we came from," like thousands of years ago, but it's definitely grown out of that. As I mentioned last night, I have a Sagittarius Moon and you cannot tell me I can't change something because then I

---

[6] *Light on Life: An Introduction to the Astrology of India*, Hart de Fouw and Robert Svoboda, Lotus Press, 2003.

have no reason to get out of bed in the morning. [group claps] And I'm acerbic and bitter, a bear and a bore.

Right now we're talking about the karma that is just what you're carrying. There is a whole other category of karma between people and there's a whole national karma, ethnic and religious group karma, and then the human collective karma which is what I think you mentioned with the collective unconscious kind of collective thing. There are all these different levels. We are focusing this weekend on the individual level but you can apply the principles of *group or individual needs to learn about certain theme, group or individual then draws experiences to manifest the theme and learn*. So you can apply it to all these greater things. Djehuty goes into this when he talks about genocide in the channeled book *Understanding Loss and Death*, and national karma, group identity, religious karma that explains why a group might create attempted or the reality of genocide. All the souls in that group have decided to learn together about this. It's interesting to read about this in the book. And there's this whole human general collective, which is the collective unconscious that is becoming conscious because people are choosing to heal the past, get multidimensional, allow these things to happen and connect to soul – all that stuff. In some of the conversations we have with you as individuals, we may talk about some relationship karma because some stuff will come up naturally, but this individual thing is where I want to stay for now.

Glenna: Is it your view that it starts at the individual level? I mean I know we're experiencing it all at once but I'm wondering if … my personal experience has been so important to get in touch with my own in order to really see the bigger picture. What's your view on that?

Tom: Yeah. I mean, any national or ethnic or cultural group is made up of individuals who are sparks or slivers of the Divine intending to learn, and they happen to share a syllabus in this life. So yes. But it is also really important to explore that group thing because of the group victimization and group identity and all that garbage, too. But it all starts with individuals. You can sit down with every soul associated with a human who perished in the Armenian genocide in the early 20th century – you could sit down with every single soul and see they share that in common but it is the individual soul's choice.

So, I tell my friend the big thing. The friend says, "get out of my life." The note, "when I'm honest with my friend about what's really important to me; when I reveal my heart; when I share my truth, I'm rejected" – something like this – some belief. Then I carry this knot with the label and then of course I'm drawing the people who need to learn the opposite side of the coin or the exact same thing. And repeating what you sow. To end this we have to come to a point not of never revealing our truth or staying away from people, or not talking or withdrawing, or wishing I didn't have to live so I wouldn't have to feel this pain – which is where a lot of people go – but changing your mind about why some painful experience in the past happened. As we get down into the layers and are dusting off the little pieces, then we rewrite history – relabel those knots – which allows those knots to dissolve. So for Glenna, the not vacuuming is not that she's a sloppy slut or whatever you said –

Group: A lazy slut.

Tom: A lazy slut. The fact is – and I remember telling you that and I remember feeling joy that you were going to grasp this because what a big deal for Saturn in the 1st house square the nodes – like, what a big deal. Actually, you're a woman who chose not to vacuum. And the relief that you feel when you get that. So this emotional archaeology is going down a list of all the things that, you know, your heart hurts about – the self-judgment, resentment of others – all that stuff. And one by one, changing your mind about why it happened. It changes the label on the knot or the file. I was doing a channeling thing by Djehuty a couple of months ago about this and he was saying that there is a file cabinet, a giant file cabinet in your psyche – meaning in your energy field – and it is jam-packed full of mislabeled files. [group laughs]

Glenna: One is labeled "lazy slut," right?

Tom: That's right! "Not doing the housework before the client = lazy slut." That's what it says in all-caps on that little label machine label that's on the tab on the folder. So when you pick up that file, which you did on the phone with me – you accessed the emotion.

Glenna: The gleeful part was when I got the razor blade out and got that label off and just put "woman who has chosen not to vacuum."

Tom: Then you'll find that there's another drawer up there that's empty, and it's reality. That situation that happened this morning happened this morning. And you let the file go – it doesn't mean anything anymore.

Annette: An empty file drawer.

Glenna: I like the imagery of that.

Tom: And then eventually this one empties out and this one fills up and you realize you can use the whole cabinet for refiling.

Now, when you get this information and you really take it in and we're talking about your personal charts, every single day you will have the opportunity to refile. Dozens of things. Last night we talked about Chiron and examples of expecting rejection: "I will not be loved if I do this; if I express this part of myself." We can put a label on that for now: "expecting rejection." Well, you know, mine's in the 7th so I have this thing about initiating relationship. A man had that ball cap on and I wouldn't have wanted to go over and tell him that was my favorite team – I don't want to do that because I might be expecting rejection with Chiron in the 7th. Every single day I have the opportunity to initiate conversation with somebody I don't know – every single day I have that opportunity. So probably each day, 3 to 40 times a day, I have an opportunity to maintain an old label on the file or to let it go. It's not letting go as in pushing it out of your awareness and deciding it's not important. Letting it go as in picking up the file – feeling that feeling – and saying, "You know what? That's not what's happening." Because when somebody did reject me it was painful in the past, it really had nothing to do with me.[7] That's the truth of it. That's the Chiron-in-the-7th house truth: how other people treat you has nothing to do with you. So I have that choice every single day with my South Node, South Node ruler, Pluto square Jupiter, Pluto in the 12th, Pluto in Libra, Venus square the nodes, Chiron in the 7th – I have that opportunity every day with every belief that I have. Some days I don't leave the house and don't see anybody, so maybe that's a free day. But all the time I'm dealing with people I have the opportunity.

With what we're here to talk about, the intention is to plant a seed so that you catch every single little belief that you carry. We're going to talk about the big ones, or the big categories of them, anyway. So not every single one but we're going to talk about the major categories. But this is, as far as I'm concerned, the way forward for any of us. Speaking for myself, just to give you a potential sneak preview of where a person can go with this, it's being aware all the time of the beliefs that guide me, being aware that every single decision I make is guided by a belief *or* it is a choice in the present moment.

Annette: Can you talk a little more about intention? Right before you brought up intention I was there, but

---

[7] Chiron in the birth chart can indicate in what part of life a person is hypersensitive to rejection.

intention is a little confusing because is it always intended? Is there such a thing as unintended?

Tom: Are you talking about the soul's intention?

Annette: [nods]

Tom: Okay. What seems unintended is something you're simply not aware of that the soul has said it will do. So the soul says, "This is what I'm learning" – and this is Divine Law, actually. That sets the world in motion. But you're not aware of it. So let's go back to my example of trust, fairness, and balance – being honest with a friend. Maybe it's the other side of the coin and somebody lies to me and I find out about it and am deflated: "That was unexpected. That's not what I set out to experience." Well that's not what my conscious personality set out to experience. The soul learned through that experience just like it would from being able to trust somebody and having my personal truth received with love. The soul learned. That's why when we learn about what the soul is intending, we can adopt those as our intentions as well, and then that brings in conscious choice. Because if I know that my soul is intending to learn about honesty in relationship, if I know that, then I can approach my relationships in a new way.

Now, when you use an energy consciously, you never feel used by it. Everybody's got every symbol in the chart. Every single person has every single energy. We try to stay away from the ones that represent what has hurt us or is related to what hurts us. So most of us have something left out in our journeys, which looks like trying not to do or be

47

that thing. So if we look at it and get that this is what the soul is trying to get done by our experiencing that, then you can change the label on the file of the bad experience that happened when you were 8 with your mom – and then you can actually be present with it, present with whatever's happening. But aligning your personality's intentions with your soul's intentions is Divine empowerment. Because then your conscious personality is no longer fighting what your soul is trying to do. Your soul is a portion of God.

Annette: When you get to that point there is no intention.

Tom: Right. It's just what's happening. It's already in play and you don't have to say, "I'm going in this direction come hell or high water" – it's more like, "I feel I'm headed to Yakima to teach a workshop – hmm – okay, let's do that. Let's call Candace and set up details." Because that's the preset intention of the soul.

Anne: So for example, what if you find yourself in relationship with a person who you are aware has been abandoned several times in this life? Is it reasonable to assume that he's setting himself up to be abandoned by you?

Tom: Yes, and then you have a choice about how you participate in his story. I mean, he always has a choice on how the story is unfolding but if he's unconscious of it, and you just said that so you're already conscious of his story at least to some degree, right? Maybe not all the details but you know what it is. He is a powerful, Divine creator with a soul setting out on a mission to create that experience and he's drawn you – you have the choice of how you're going to participate. The ball is thrown – he's throwing this ball: "This is what you're going to do for me." You can pluck the ball out of midair and say, "Actually, I saw you throw the ball. I understand that that's something that you throw. I would like to have a different level of conversation about it." And then that person can either embrace you or remove himself from your life. I'm a fan of the metaconversation – whatever's happening, can we talk about why and how it is happening and why you're creating that? Just because I can't deal with subtext. [clapping from group and comments] I'm getting applause for that – thank you.

Recently I had a conversation with another person in which I asked, "What is the bottom-line thing that you can't deal with?" And we exchanged them. I realized that I always set out to do stuff like that but I don't always do it. I did it and it felt awesome because I was able to say, "This is my bottom-line thing that freaks me out, stresses me out, and that I would hold resentment about." And the other person said, "Oh, here's mine: this thing I can't do, that would stress me out." How empowering is that, you know? Whether it's a new relationship or one that's been going on for years or decades, to have that … But with the work that I do, I can't avoid people's underlying motivations and how I sense what their energy fields are up to and what their souls are trying to get done. It's a different way of having relationships but with more consciousness, more awareness. Look around at everyone else in the room and feel what everyone else is feeling, right now, after I just said that. [pause] It went like this, the course of the couple of sentences: "what's he gonna say??" Then "ahhh…"

Glenna: That happened earlier when Candace came in and said, "Can I be honest with you?"[8]

Tom: Oh, it did happen, didn't it? And I said, "Please."

Glenna: And that was my experience, I was like, "Oh, you're going to say it? Good." Because it was here already. And then once she said it and Tom responded then it sort of dissipated.

Tom: That's being in the present. She recognized in that moment that that's what she needed to say and you're checking in. But you've surrounded yourself with people who want to have that level of dialogue, even if we're not all practiced at it we know how important it is.

Jillian: And we had this conversation the other day about how sometimes you're conscious of your own subtext in the moment, sometimes you're not but you're conscious of the other person's subtext and it takes a mutual awareness of that in order to get at what's really going on.

Glenna: That's an important point. I appreciate that so much when I'm feeling it but not said, and then when someone brings it.

---

[8] The day began with a last-minute cancellation from someone who had committed to the workshop. Candace came in just before we started and needed to get the frustration off her chest before we proceeded.

Jillian: Because sometimes it can be scary. You're not aware of your own subtext and then maybe you don't feel you can express it because of some of the beliefs that you've attached to it.

Candace: What you just said was, "I believe in *meta*conversation" – isn't that what you said?

Tom: I think so.

Candace: And you said you believe it's much better to get below the subtext and actually say, "I see the subtext" – can we just bring it out into some light? It will feel much better if we bring it up into a space where it can be embraced.

Tom: And that is reflecting interacting with each other without our karma. I have this idea – this thing is guiding my participation in this conversation with you. We're sitting around and my belief is guiding it. So I'm allowing my karma, my beliefs about past experience, to determine how I interact with you right now.

Group: Exactly.

Tom: So this whole conversation about karma – yeah, you can repeat what you sowed in 1320s Egypt! You totally can. I can keep my mouth shut when I'm inspired by something you just said because I'm afraid; because something happened in like 1720s Virginia.

Glenna: A lot of it is related to fear, isn't it?

Candace: Isn't all of it?

Tom: Candace, were you afraid when you came in and said that you needed to say that? [gets nod] Exactly! But she's making it a practice of identifying the fear and then making a decision on is this the right day to do something about it or not – is this the right moment? Not all of us are going to jump on this: "This is my subtext: ..." We don't need to do it all the time.

Glenna: I love that she also asked permission if it was okay ...

Tom: In this space that we're creating together – right. And she's getting to know me in a certain way where I always want the truth.

Candace: And that's because I want to be able to be honest. In this lifetime I want it to be safe to be honest.

Tom: Well, so obviously you've created that.

Glenna: With the two sides of the coin that you were talking about – I'm having this epiphany and want to tell you about it. When you're feeling that tension like with a square, when you say, "Ooh, that part of me I see reflected in you that makes me uncomfortable about myself ..." But then it's invited into this dialogue where we have to feel safe enough, which would depend on this context, to be able to have what happened there with you, to say "First of all, I have something to share – is it okay for me to share?" And you're reflecting it, so there's the oneness in that as you can get past that fear then there's that invitation to connect and clear. It's almost like a little factory especially now with the acceleration [of the evolution of consciousness] that's going, "Let's just take care of each thing in turn and let it go."

Tom: So I want to tell you the side you don't know yet about that interaction, which was what was happening in

52

me – because I want to show you the other side of the coin. I have the opportunity – and one of my commitments with my relationship with Candace is to take the opportunity, because I believe in her and she believes in me and it's a good source of feedback … The hesitancy that a part of her always feels about speaking up makes a part of me nervous and unhappy because I'm not always forthright. So I see the hesitancy to speak the truth and a part of me would be inclined to be impatient with her because I'm feeling that. That's my karma. So she says, "I want to say something" and I say, "Bring it!" because I'm choosing not to perpetuate my karma of regret for not speaking up about my truth – regret, judgment, the karma or belief that I assigned to what happened when I spoke my truth and it turned out crappy, when I in a group said, "This is what I need to say" and somebody said, "Get the hell out!" or "Who do you think you are?" Or, "I'm getting ready to teach this workshop – can you just shut your hole?" All these things that could have happened with others telling me they don't want to hear it.

But I resonate with that and I say now, "I strive to speak the truth, too." It's really important to me and part of the dynamic I happen to have with Candace is that I can let the part of her that always hesitates, I can judge her because I'm judging myself or I can allow that she has something to say. This present way of communicating offers the chance to get rid of all the karma, just to get that it's not all actually true (the beliefs from the past). What I think or fear might happen doesn't have to happen. We're talking about it in rather intimate terms – in the space of this workshop in which we're creating a space together and connecting – but it can happen on an individual basis every single day. Like at a gas station the other day in Oregon, the guy who was pumping the gas was wonderful. He's chit-chatty and smiley, smiley, smiley, and he asks me about where I'm headed and I tell him to teach a workshop. He asks about it and I don't usually tell random people about this stuff but I told him it's astrology, spirituality, and metaphysics. And there was this turning point and he said, "Is that biblical?" Now, I don't know where this guy is coming from. But with Chiron in the 7th, I don't want to tell him. So I told him it's not biblical but it's helping people understand themselves better, connecting to soul, and it's bringing soul into conscious awareness and understanding why the soul has chosen to become this person. And he said, "Oh, that's really cool. I was just curious if it was biblical. I don't care about religion." But I had no idea – and it's a risk. I can let that guy be who he is and if he says, "I don't go for all that nonsense and I'm a biblical kind of guy," or whatever, then it's not about me and my work is still pretty cool – I still feel it's pretty rad. So the choice in every interaction is to choose in this example not to expect rejection.

This teaching on karma is so different from what we have picked up. When we teach it this way, it has so much potential to be empowering. It puts a mantle of responsibility on you to watch your thoughts and to choose to create reality how you want, but it's not this, "I'm having a bad day and that person lied to me, and it must be my karma – poor me."

*   *   *

Michael changed his shirt during the break.

Tom: Is it because I said people with black shirts can't be trusted?

Michael: I changed my shirt because I was afraid you would not be able to trust me.

Tom: Thank you.

Michael: I just got a little too hot in my black shirt. So I thought I'd just get another shirt.

Tom: Because I also have a thing about not trusting people who wear Hawaiian or floral shirts. And also beige, yellow, orange, banana, and/or like sand-colored shirts. I can't trust people with leaf patterns on their shirts.

Summer: And he gets to know not to take it personally.

Tom: Exactly!

Candace: You can have compassion for his limited belief system.

Tom: Okay. We're going to wrap up the karma thing before we get into the elements in the birth chart that speak to all of this stuff. Are there questions, comments, or thoughts or derisions about what we've done so far? Is everything clear?

Summer: Is it as easy as looking at the old energy that might be stuck, holding compassion for it, understanding, love for it – and growing from that experience and allowing that energy to go back to Source? Just by viewing it in a different way?

Tom: Yes, and also being willing to feel all we can feel and not judging the fact that we're feeling it. Because some of the things that come up are intense and you sometimes don't want to be intense or seen to be intense. You don't want to take up all the room you expect you might take up if you express all this emotion right now. You might not want to offend others with the intensity of your feeling – what you're feeling might be rage. So what you said plus acknowledging the reality of the feelings that are so intense that sometimes we do try to block them. Regarding where you just said you were,[9] there were people there willing to experience ecstasy in front of other people. Grief, anger, joy, ecstasy, pleasure, inspiration, the joy that comes from synchronicity, resentment – all these things that, if you were filled with them, you could deeply affect other people. So, being willing to feel all we can feel, observing the patterns that we have (the beliefs), and being willing to change the filing system labels and let it go. But what tends to happen is that we get overtaken by the emotion we have. So the person backstabbed me 30 years ago and I never got over it. What happens when someone seems to perhaps be heading that way with me now – you know, my guard will get raised because it's trying to

---

[9] Summer had said during the break that she was recently returned from Burning Man and had a wonderful sense of community because she could express herself fully there and connect with others doing the same.

protect a feeling that I have and I might be afraid of having it come out. Some people will throw their feelings around because they don't know what else to do with it or they need the attention or acknowledgment or validation: "This feeling's real and if you recoil from it I know that I'm real; I know that that feeling is actually happening." Maybe I grew up in a house where no one talked about feelings. But most of us don't do that. Most of us don't want – well, we might even be able to talk about rage and grief, resentment and anger, but we got filled with it. We don't want to carry it to somebody. We want to hide it.

All of the things that parts of us might label as ugly – that's also karma and beliefs. *Anger is unacceptable. Resentment isn't appropriate. This is what a good girl does. This is how big boys act.* The tips from the Chiron talk last night about getting grounded and allowing ourselves to feel what we're feeling but then being conscious, remaining conscious – this is one of the keys to changing karma. As we talked about it it might make total sense to your mind, it's resonating in your heart and perhaps other energy centers in your body and you can be committed to doing that. But what happens is that you're filled with an emotion that overtakes you. That's what actually happens when we confront the deep karma. We want detachment but not distance in order to do manage that effectively.

Maybe some of the conversations we have here will touch certain parts of us that are difficult to face. Tender parts come up and when we talk about it in this kind of context it can be experienced as tender because you're not going to feel threatened. As you're out in the world it can feel threatening when somebody else might push that pain button that I carry and then I have to hit the karma button of what it meant – you know, everyone is pressing each other's buttons. So it actually is that simple except that you're a complex energetic being who has a cache of emotion that you carry around. I can attest that it helps to understand what the soul is trying to experience through me because then I can catch myself and have that context, and I can see things coming in certain relationships, and I can talk about it as I can smell something coming. It's like a setup for karmic growth and then I can choose how to respond to it. The theme *will* come to me because I am resonating and vibrating: *theme, come to me*. So it will come to me but I have a choice about how to respond to it.

Let's transition into talking about the symbols in the chart that we use to discern and understand karma.

The 4-step Method of Chart Analysis

Pluto

Tom: We start with Pluto.[10] In evolutionary astrology there are two main threads. One is the soul's intentions and desires and that comes from the work of Jeff Green, and the other thread is the soul's wounding, which is from the work of Steven Forrest. We could say the soul's deepest intentions and the deepest wounding. What I've learned from channeling and mediumship I've done is – and this is all reflected in *The Soul's Journey I*, so if you want the full story outside of this context, see that book – the intents and desires and the wounding are actually reflecting or part and parcel of the soul's empowerment journey, and so this is where I start with Pluto. A portion of Divinity splits itself off with the intention of forgetting temporarily (over millions of years) and ultimately remembering its Divine nature. And the point of coming here is to learn what it means to do so.

---

[10] In *The Soul's Journey I: Astrology, Reincarnation, and Karma with a Medium and Channel* Pluto appears as step 3. Its significance remains unchanged.

So why do humans exist? To figure out what it means to be human; to experience being separate, being tied to time, forgetting our Divine nature. Pluto represents the statement that the soul makes that says, "When I go to Earth and get embodied and am tied to time, and I forget my true nature, Pluto in my birth chart will represent how I seek to become empowered in that context, having forgotten my true nature." It's the soul's empowerment journey through many lives is the best way to say it.

Wherever Pluto is in the chart represents one subset of the handful of themes. I used the example earlier of some dude who my soul was on the Earth time line had Pluto in Cancer in the 10th and that's where my South Node is now, and my Pluto's in the 12th where his South Node is so that the symbols and emphases can get traded – those are major themes. In this life I have Pluto in Libra but in every single life I don't have Pluto in Libra, but I will have Pluto in some relationship with Venus whether it's in the 7th house, conjunct Venus, etc. – that's the kind of baseline. The soul seeks to become empowered as a human in the midst of this forgetfulness and that's what Pluto represents.

The intention is to become empowered. I'm one of billions. Over much of the Earth time line you don't have any concept of that but I'm one of hundreds or thousands, or perhaps millions. Now we talk about there being 7 billion people on the planet and we can maybe not even wrap our minds about what that really means but we have that number we can work with. But in other times I might be one of 4,000 or 5,000 people in my area. How much do I matter? What do I want and need? The empowerment journey as an individual is one thing but from the soul's perspective, that person has forgotten his true, Divine nature. Thus far in time-space, meaning thus far in the history of this planet and the existence of humans, in the process of this manifestation experiment we're living through, thus far – up to the end of the Mayan Calendar – we are learning about empowerment through material means and through duality.

We've all heard spiritual teachings that have to do with becoming empowered within ourselves. We've all read or heard or trafficked in those things. But we're also carrying the emotional history of having in many ways felt overpowered because we live in dualism. When the soul says, "I'm going to learn about power and strength," you are automatically going to learn about that through having it and not having it. When my friends receive my honesty with loving kindness, I'm empowered. When my friend resents me for bringing up a difficult topic, I'm disempowered. That's the history. When I work with clients – and we will discuss with your charts – you have both kinds of experiences. Candace has Saturn-Pluto in Leo in the 5th. She has experiences of speaking her truth and having mountains move: the world changes around her when she speaks her truth! And she also has experiences where she says, "This is my truth" and somebody who is more Plutonian in some way – seemingly more powerful in an external sense – comes in and says, "Your opinion doesn't quite matter that much." She has both experiences.

One of things that we do when we do this work is to find the part of you that remembers being empowered from doing the soul's work. But that's where this Pluto comes in: You already know what it feels like to do it well and to come out on top but you've been coming out on top through dualism, through duality. Many people who at this point in time who are healing Pluto issues are afraid of overpowering others so they don't want to do their Pluto.

I don't want to be the kind of person who hurt me. Most models of strength are through duality and center on people having power over each other – we don't want to do that. Some of us do but most of us don't, so we choose disempowerment to not manifest what we feel in our hearts we have to do, like the do-or-die thing – *if I don't do this thing my life will be meaningless* – that's Pluto, too. When those moments shine through that's you remembering soul, you remembering the soul's mission, what you intended. But then you're also having to deal with the stakes feeling very high because you don't want to get hurt again – that's the intentions and the pain coexisting and there's back-and-forth: *I have to do this but it hurts so much that I'm afraid to do it.* Think about the tension in your chest when you think about what you might have come to Earth to do and you can't quite let yourself do it or you have to – that's Pluto – and the soul's mandate being visible or apparent, feeling-wise.

So there's a different way to look at strength and power outside of dualism and duality. It is absolute, utter, unflinching, unashamed, unabashed self-knowledge and total self-acceptance.

Where there's a part of us sitting with a finger on a Pluto button labeled "this is going to disempower me if I have to experience it," that's waiting to press it, if you know what all parts of you are afraid of, fear, hate, and resent because of this history of being overpowered through and in duality, then you know what every part of you is about. Because you already know the loving parts. You already know the parts that want to feed other people home-made soup and be loving and kind. You love those parts! Everybody wants those parts to come out. But the part that might be angry and really apocalyptically angry at having been silenced or something – having been overpowered, trapped, ignored, having been shamed, etc. So real Pluto empowerment is absolute self-knowledge and then utter self-acceptance of what is seen.

I like giving images so I'm going to tell you about the house that is your psyche. It's a two-level house. Let's say that there are four rooms on each floor. There was an extra bedroom and you made it an office or studio. You have a window box in the kitchen where you grow begonias. You do some sprouting in the kitchen and you have a little garden outside and you keep your house tidy. But the last time you were in the basement was when you moved in and you dumped all your shit that you don't know what to do with. Those old photo albums of people with whom the relationships ended painfully but you're not sure what to do with them. Or the inheritance, the item, that came from your grandmother that reminded you of how she criticized you but you can't get rid of it because it was your grandmother and that's family and history. That kind of stuff.

Well, you almost maybe haven't cleaned out the closets since you moved in. "Well what am I going to do with this extra baseball bat? I guess I'll put it in the closet…" "What about this thing that doesn't quite work but could be fixed? I guess I'll put it in the closet, too." And then the attic. But you live in these 8 rooms and you're very happy, but there're other spaces in the house.

With this idea of the Pluto empowerment thing, what's happening is that there are parts of you within your psyche, within this house that is your psyche, who feel that they cannot live in the house with you in a joyous way because they're ugly, they're hateful, and they feel they should hide in the basement, closets, or the attic. But they're inside the house – you can't get rid of them no matter what you do.

So you have a friend over to your house, a friend you've known for 11 years. You share interests and hobbies, whatever. You're comfortable having the friend in your house but one day the friend shows up and says, "Hmm, do you have a basement here? I never even thought to ask if you have a basement here." And you're like, "[gasps]" because there's all this crap down there you didn't know what to do with and it's such a mess and you know you don't need that stuff but … And you have fear that someone's going to see what's in these places that are not in the main space. This is a Pluto fear button – we're afraid of having all these parts seen. Not to get too Scorpionic about it but other people can sometimes sense what you're afraid of. So you're available to have your fears triggered, and then you can feel disempowered when others can push your fear buttons. Real Pluto life and living is in absolute self-knowledge –

"Who's in the basement?! Is somebody hiding down there?!"

"Yes, apocalyptic anger at having been ignored and shamed at my job."

That's what calls back up from downstairs, though it might sound like this, "[grunting/growling]." And you say, "Oh, my god, that sounded like apocalyptic anger and shame ..." [group laughs] "Oh, I knew you were down there but I was just hoping that you'd leave or something so I wouldn't have to deal with you." The friend is just sitting there waiting for an answer to the question, "Do you have a basement here?" And then the friend asks, "Do you have an attic?"

Anyway. These parts of us that might be hiding out – we're afraid of people seeing them. We're afraid of the debris that we're carrying because it's nasty. But Plutonian living in a healthy way requires absolute self-knowledge.

Let's say that you're in your house and you make it a regular habit of knowing who's hiding in the basement and you're not forcing them out into the light of day or criticizing them or making it a problem. But you're like, "Yeah, you know, this part of me thinks that his or her feelings are really ugly." Just by acknowledging that, that part is known and even if that part holds on to anger, resentment, and bitterness and is still hiding, you are not keeping it out of awareness. Eventually the part comes up out of the basement and bridges are built but if you don't want to know who they are, anybody coming in your house is potentially making you afraid of being in your own house. If you have a relationship with these parts and you acknowledge them, the question of if you have a basement isn't a problem. You can let it be fine that it's used for storage and you might not know what to do with all of what's down there, and you're aware of it. Someone saying they want to go there – it won't be a big deal because it won't be a secret. We're naturally inclined to be emotional and psychological detectives but when you know what's in the house, other people can't inadvertently or intentionally push the buttons of fear that you might carry. You acknowledge that parts of you carry fear. When I told you about my experience in the conversation with Candace earlier, I said that part of her that wants to hesitate when speaking the truth makes the resonant part of me nervous. Well, I know who's hiding out in the closet. I know who's back there. So you say that and I remember that I have this part of me and then I respond to you in the moment.

This is a lot to do with Pluto because this involves power-over and power-under. Pluto is often said to be about our subconscious – the basement. As we talk about your charts we're going to be talking about who's in your

66

basement, who's in the attic, and who's hiding in the closets. If you've done work with me, you've seen that, we've talked about that at least a little bit.

Michael: Pluto is said to be about hidden agendas?

Tom: Yes.

Michael: So we need to know a little about each thing? Each part represents a hidden agenda?

Tom: That's it. In the basement, if a part of you wants or needs something but you don't acknowledge it, then that's a hidden agenda. This part of me needs to express my anger at having been ignored but that's a hidden agenda because I don't acknowledge it. As soon as I say, "Yeah, I've got this basement and I've got this part of me hanging out there and he's mad," then it's not hidden anymore. But we have shame about what we think is ugly within us, and that's the history of Pluto in our lives because when somebody overpowers you in some life, it hurts. And lots of times anger grows out of pain. All anger covers over pain but we don't always get angry after getting hurt. Lots of times we do. For intentionally being ignored or not being heard, there's an anger there and it looks like something that might be really nasty, violent – who knows what will happen because I was really hurt by that. It's a survival thing. I feel like I have to lash out in order to protect myself – it's a survival thing. And everybody's got that in Pluto though the theme is different.

There's a lot to say about Pluto but for the context of changing karma this is where I wanted to go with it. You have empowering and disempowering experiences over your multilife journey and the trick is to acknowledge the disempowerment, change the karma which is the meaning you've assigned to why those things happened, and to choose to feed the part that actually can be empowered through doing this.

Michael: If Mercury's communication, what is Pluto?

Tom: I would say integrity, honesty, empowerment, and truth – strength – inner, unshakable strength would be one thing. Because when you know about all the parts in the basement and all that stuff, nobody can stop you, nobody wants to. They want to see you shine. They want to see you bring this complex light. You walk into the room and you're like, "This is who I am. This is what I'm about. Do you want to play with me? No? That's cool." But it's not apologetic about being strong, and that inspires people in my experience.

When we look in the chart, Pluto represents the soul's empowerment journey. The house is the arena of life through which empowerment will be explored. The sign is how that arena of life will be approached and also about its motivation, what drives the action. But the house is where the action is and the sign is how things are happening and why.

The aspects to Pluto represent the intentions that the soul has to learn about certain energies in certain relationships. We will get specific in charts but the general thing is that aspects affect the soul's journey but they are the soul's intention to learn about certain energies in certain relationships. I don't want to get too specific but I want to give you one example. Let's say that natally somebody has Mars square Pluto, about 90 degrees. That indicates friction. Most of us would look at a chart and say, "I have Mars square Pluto – all these problems with violence, abuse, fights, arguments – argh." But to look at why the soul would intend to have Mars square Pluto – there's an intention there. The soul says, "For my mission, I'm going to learn about Mars by receiving friction from it." That's the soul's intention. That person might have been abused as a child, or that person might have been mugged as an adult and really traumatized. That person could have experienced a lot of negative Mars stuff and the emotion from that is what we carry, what we're filled with and triggered by but the soul's intention is to learn about Mars through being squared by it. "My soul's mission will receive friction. I may not be able to get where I'm going all the time because I'm getting knocked off course from left field, knocked off balance by Mars." The soul intends it! That's what I mean with the aspects to Pluto. We'll get specific in charts but I want to give you that note. But I do get that question from clients. They say they're working on an abuse issue and we talk about it but then 20 minutes later I bring them into talking about what the soul's intention is. And people sometimes get very angry because the buttons are pressed: "I would never sign up to be abused." I tell them they're right that but that they signed up to learn about power and aggression. We'll get into that more later.

Michael: You brought up something interesting. I would not have thought that my soul would intend to have these complications in life, but it has decided to have this struggle. I would say my intelligence would not choose this.

Tom: Of course not.

Michael: Like you said, somebody gets angry at something, saying, "I wouldn't choose this! I'm too intelligent to do this kind of complication."

Tom: I had a client with whom I worked quite a bit through readings and coaching for I guess maybe 15 or 16 months. All the channeled perspectives about responsibility I used in my work with her just like I do and would with everybody. And then she said something in a recent session and I told her the best explanation for that question is in one of these channeled books so she bought two of them. I explained what each of the three is about and she bought two. And then she got them in the mail and she read them and she decided that I had lost my mind.

I told her they were channeled, so everything in them except for the introduction and the acknowledgments is not mine. I thought maybe she didn't know what channeling really was but what happened is that she probably went straight to the section on sexual violence, which says that your soul is creating violence to serve a learning purpose, and it pressed the button. It pressed the deeply painful cache of emotions where the thing is still swollen and throbbing, where the pain is ever-present and real. Based on the ensuing communications, I think her mind jumped in and said, "There is no way anybody could say that somebody chooses that." But she'd been digging the teachings all that time, until she read the undistilled version, the direct version in that text, and then that energetically got through. Anyway, I was the greatest astrologer on Earth for 15 months. I was like the best spiritual teacher on the planet until the button got pushed, and then it's very clear that I have lost my mind.

So this responsibility thing is a huge deal and I always preface it. If I give a talk it's usually an hour or two, or a phone call or something, it's kind of brief, but you're getting this extended talk so you're getting the real prefatory notes – the disclaimers and the qualifiers. You're getting all of them because we have to deal with the difficult emotions but yeah, we chose it. And it is hard. Everybody's got something that is very painful, at least one thing definitely but it can be a category of thing, that appears as if somebody has done something to us. Because through our human eyes it looks that way.

Glenna: [voice breaking a little] If a person is willing to own that empowerment – listen to my voice, my 5th chakra – let me speak my truth here – that you're talking about here, forcing us to come out of victim mode... Suddenly I'm imagining myself as that client, thinking, "Oh I can't handle that so let me make it about you – you lost your mind." And I don't have to take responsibility for whatever I have to do to help this pain go through me and for me to let go of it. There's all that karma. If I just make it about you being nuts, I can stop right there. And that victim stance giving way to that empowered stance: "Ah, I chose that. What does my soul want to do with that? To continue that loop or take it in this empowered manifestation and move it on?"

Tom: And what we confront in that moment, what we end up finding, is the intensity of the identification of why the victimhood happened – why the thing happened. The intensity of identification. When we talk about karma, beliefs, and the knots with the labels we're talking about identity based in what has happened to us.

Glenna: Assigning a lot of meaning to that and holding it, identifying with it.

Tom: That's right. We started that talk last night with the question, "What is a human?" What I didn't talk about at that point but I will talk about it now: Are you the sum of your experiences? Are you someone who is lied to? Are you somebody who is controlled by others? Are you somebody who is afraid to speak? Or are you a Divine being who is trying to figure out how the hell to be human in a healthy way?

If we let it, that leads us to be compassionate with ourselves about every single thing, if we're willing to give up the identity of "I'm terrible" or whatever. And it then leads us to be compassionate with everybody else for anything that they're experiencing and having going on. In the moment with that client I was not compassionate and now two weeks later I'm able to be compassionate. And we were talking about subtext earlier. There was something she wasn't telling me about why this was happening. I told you she thought I was nuts and at first she wouldn't tell me why, just putting up this weird energy, and I got stressed because I don't do well when people project on me or withhold information. I freak out when people project, actually. It's like a real Achilles heel and I've been working on it. But Pluto in Libra in the 12th – just can't deal with that … so far.

Not everybody in every life is going to have that Pluto fear button pressed a lot because most of us construct around avoiding having it pressed. Think of Pluto in Leo in the 5th. How much energy have you, Candace, spent not speaking, not saying what you need to say or expressing your opinions? With Pluto in Libra in the 12th, how much energy have I spent hiding my interest in creating justice? I have done it a lot because the stakes are so high. The stakes are so high that I'm not always sure how to be in that space because it makes me vulnerable if I'm still dealing with the pain.

So most of us construct our lives around not having Pluto triggered. And then we might go through a transformative period. We might have a transit of Pluto or a transit or progression to Pluto and say, "Whoa. I've really left something out or really denied something." I'll mention another client of mine who has Pluto in the 8th house, with a loaded 8th house in Virgo and Leo, and she recently took the family healing e-course. Pluto is transiting her Ascendant – natal Pluto in the 8th, which can tend to be a little more quiet; intense under the surface but not always out loud. It's transited all the way to her Ascendant and suddenly she doesn't want to put up with anything from anybody. But she's very kind and generous and gentle. I told her that the parts of her that are mad about 8th house stuff: "you're being invited now to own that because it's on your Ascendant – you can't help but express it." Helping her navigate that transit involves changing her context for natal Pluto from 8th-house quiet to Ascendant-based expression. She's doing great work with it but she said something like, "So what you're basically saying is that whatever's going on in that 8th house I can't avoid now because transiting Pluto's at the 1st house?" I said yes and that was empowering for her because she's ready to make changes.

But where's the identity with what's happened? Are you the sum of what's happened to you? Are you your emotional history? Are you your family history? Are you the experiences you've had in your career? Are you your friendships, are you the marriage that you chose? Or are you the marriages you refused? Are you opportunities that you lost or sacrificed?

That's the intro on Pluto for our weekend together. That underlies everything in a given life. Each of these first three symbols – Pluto, South Node, and the South Node ruler represent aspects of identity below conscious personality. It's traditional in Western astrology to look at a chart and go straight for Sun, Moon, and Ascendant, and then Mercury, Venus, and Mars, and then Jupiter and Saturn and on out. To look at things personal versus impersonal. Looking at the chart in this way I'm describing cuts to the quick of the soul's intentions and journey. The conscious personality is a set of tools to deal with that karma. It does make a difference if your Sun is opposing your South Node, which means that your conscious identity now needs to oppose your past. All those things matter but Sun, Moon, rising, and inner planets aspects of personality and levels of identity in the present moment that are above this rich, complex, lava undercurrent of emotional stuff from all these lives. That's why I go straight to Pluto and the nodes: because I want to know who you really are, not who you feel like you are on Tuesday but I want to know where your soul has been and what you *really* feel.

South Node of the Moon

Tom: The nodes are points that are the intersections of the Moon's orbit around the Earth and the Earth's orbit around the Sun. The planes are not parallel – the orbital planes intersect. Where the Moon goes up in its orbital plane is the North Node and where it goes down is the South Node. So these are points and not planets or bodies.

The South Node of the Moon is a repository of emotional memories from the past, from other lives but including this life. This symbol in a chart represents the choice of the soul to develop a starting place in any given life. The family that the soul is born into in any given life will be represented by the South Node. It reflects comfort

75

zones and habit patterns from many, many lives. It's a conscious choice of the soul: "I have to be trained how to be human so I'm going to pick a family that will teach me *this* way of being." It doesn't mean that if you have an Aquarius South Node that everyone in your family has an Aquarius Sun or Moon or something. It means that the themes of the South Node determine much of the experience there. It might be that they're all Tauruses but they're all scientists, and that would fit with an Aquarian energy, or inventors or politicians or something. Again we're back to the idea of themes; it's not all literal.

It's what you are unconsciously comfortable with. You become conscious of it eventually because you realize you'd rather stay there, in that corner of the house, than somewhere else. Habit patterns, comfort zones, preferences, which can all lead to ruts because it's not challenging to be there. Even if it's painful to be there, you know it.

Michael: So habit energies would come from there?

Tom: That's where you are inclined to habituate – it's where you're drawn. You would rather stay there – you're comfortable there. Habits come from all places but we're talking about the soul's conditioning. It's actually a lens that you will tend to see the world through.

Michael: And that's pretty strong.

Tom: Yes, it's very strong. I have a South Node in Cancer so I will tend to see the world through a Cancerian lens, which is lunar or Moon-related. I will see everything as being about emotion. I mean, look at what I do for a living – with the emotional archaeology. Last night's talk was "Chiron and Human Evolution." Well, what's that evolution about? Dealing with our feelings in a new way. I see the world that way. That's where I'm most comfortable.

Routinely in life we are challenged to go to the opposite side, to the North Node. I'll tell you a little about it now but I'm not going to tell you everything quite yet. Basically, you're comfortable in the South Node. Naturally life will bring you opportunities to grow in new directions and that's usually the North Node. But we always prefer the South Node even if it's terrible; we prefer our comfort zone even if we're unhappy – at least it's familiar.

They are always opposite. Opposite house, opposite sign. 180 degrees around the wheel in position in the chart but also quality of experience. One we cling to and one we probably have prejudices against. We want to stay in the South but need to grow toward the North. We'll cover this soon but I want to mention this opposition, this contrast.

We do consider house, sign, and aspects to the South Node. The house is the major arena of life where we're conditioned to feel comfortable. The sign is the way of being, the mode of being, the lens we live through. In a lot of the work that I do I'm confronting people's fears of change and they will want to retreat to what's familiar, their South Node. Like with me, with a Capricorn North Node, someone might say to me, "Be realistic, be mature, get up at the same time every day" – something like that – and I will automatically revert to in an unconscious way a la knee-jerk reaction revert to Cancerian-lens stuff: "But I'm feeling, I don't want to do that. I'm feeling emotions, blah blah blah." And someone says, "Be consistent," and I respond with, "But I'm feeling this today." It's just that I prefer it. I can get myself there but the pull of habit is strong.

Because the South Node represents the environments we're raised in we will tend to see the world that way. Family is a microcosm of how we later project reality on the world. If dad's a tyrant, what happens when you're in high school and there's the principal? That person is probably a tyrant or seen by you to be one – you create the world around you based on that habit pattern and comfort zone. With Pluto I asked the question, "What is a soul really trying to get done here as a human?" Now with the South Node we ask, "What does that person think is happening around him or her? How does that person see the world?"

South Node Ruler

Tom: And now we're going to go to the 3rd part of it which is the South Node ruler by sign. If we're talking about a Taurus South Node we're looking to Venus as the ruler. If Capricorn, Saturn is the ruler. That's another level of unconscious identity. I go in a specific direction with it where some other evolutionary astrologers would say it's another level of information or another cache of information that would help us learn more about the karmic story. What I do is treat it as the person's preferred role within the environment described by the South Node. If the South Node is in Capricorn the environment is Capricorny – blah, blah, blah. We can tell a whole story about how the person sees the world. Wherever Saturn is in the chart – because Saturn rules Capricorn – that's a deeper layer of identity. Who is that person within the preferred context? When we get into details with this it explains black sheep and never fitting in. It explains when people are just like their family. You can have the South Node in one sign and the ruler in square aspect to it – the person will be in friction with his or her environment. The role will seem to be about friction with the people he or she comes from. It explains so much.

Again, house, sign, and aspect. House: what part of life is this person most comfortable operating or performing in? Sign: How is this person showing up, what skills and motivations does this person have? This level of identity about who are you within the context you find yourself in? Special skills, motivations, interests, and desires but it's also qualities and traits people naturally see in you. You actually get appointed to roles in your family environment that are explained by the South Node ruler in your chart.

Michael: Whoa.

Tom: Yes!

Candace: Can you repeat that?

Tom: You can look at the South Node ruler to understand the roles people are even unwittingly appointed to within their family systems. You could have the South Node wherever and the ruler in Libra and that person is automatically relied on as the mediator. Special skills – what does the person bring to the table even if he or she is unaware of it? For me, I was not relied upon in my family to do the South Node ruler's thing but I naturally showed up with the interest. Often people are appointed.

Candace: Can you give us an example?

Tom: Yeah. We're not yet into your charts so I'll use me as an example. My South Node's in Cancer in the 10th house, so I have people in my family history who are very interested in public service and sometimes shepherding people – that kind of Cancerian care giving, nurturing. And that's the family history side of it. I have past lives of seeking to do the same thing. But the South Node ruler is in Sagittarius – extremely different energy. So I come from people who are in their emotions whether for good or bad or they're shut down for good or bad, but I'm Sagittarian – I'm like, "Can we talk about something exciting? Is there any reason I can have hope about anything?" But I'm surrounded by people who are dealing with their emotions.

Group: Or not.

Tom: Or not dealing with them, right. But "my family system is defined by a relationship to emotions" is a great way to say it. And I am additionally defined by my need to have faith in something or to explore new horizons, gather new experience, or make noise and find joy.

Candace: Have an adventure.

Tom: Have an adventure. Travel. Another way of looking at the Cancer South Node is that the family system is defined by an attempt at stability and consistency and I'm Sagittarius: I'm trying to *go* somewhere. "Who are you people to expect me to come home for holidays?! I have an adventure I'm unfolding!" So the South Node ruler here is in fact quincunx the sign of the South Node, so I feel in a way at odds. A quincunx is a very uncomfortable relationship. You feel you can't be in the same room together. It's one of the symbols that explains my need for freedom from family. My mom's single request – revealing my family history – one of her deepest needs is to have her children call her on religious holidays and wish her a happy thing or a somber thing – whatever the holiday's about. And I cannot do it. I tried for years. Every time I made that call – and I can feel my throat starting to close up now – I cannot do it. Eventually I told her that I love her and I cannot do that for my own reasons that I'm not fully processed about. My South Node ruler explains in part explains a very uncomfortable relationship with the people I come from.

Other examples: South Node ruler conjunct the South Node – can be in lock step with the family. "We can finish each other's sentences; ha ha ha, game is night is so fun! We've been taking family vacations together. My parents are 80 and I'm 60 and we go on vacation together." It can indicate a level of cohesion: "we feel like we belong together."

South Node ruler square the South Node: "I cannot stop arguing with my parents. I don't fit. I can't leave. I have to leave." That kind of struggle of belonging versus needing to leave.

South Node ruler opposing the South Node: You are running emotional, energetic, intellectual software that is the opposite of your people. That's a black-sheep thing. Just never fit – never belonged. So think about that when you look at charts. Are you thinking about somebody you know.

Group: Yes.

Tom: That person will struggle with being a black sheep or not being accepted. Whether by conscious choice or not, this describes that your soul set out about family by feeling that you can't fit in with them.

All of this is the result of me asking the Ascended Master, "Can you tell me about soul and how intentions show up in the birth chart?" These are the answers.

Candace: Thank you, Ascended Master!

Tom: Yeah.

One thing that happens that I'll touch on here and get into more deeply later has to do with the aspects to the South Node ruler. You might try to help someone see how to get more Saturnian in order to bring some issue in his or life into balance but if the South Node ruler is squared by Saturn, he or she will have uncomfortable experiences with Saturn energy in many lives and might be hesitant to become Saturnian. The karma – or beliefs – that go with being squared by a planet can have us resisting strengthening that energy within us until the karma is resolved.

Candace: I'm wondering about the opposition to the South Node. For example a South Node in Capricorn with the ruler Saturn in Cancer, in the 7th.

Tom: So it's on the North Node?

Candace: It might be. So the person would feel that any kind of nurturing authority perhaps is what they can't get to?

Tom: It might be that way.

Candace: They don't believe that they really are a nurturing authority or that it is allowable.

Tom: Yes. Because it hasn't happened before. The soul has said it needs to learn about family by not feeling connected to them.

Candace: Perhaps, "I feel I don't belong."

Tom: Yes, or you have the Capricorn South Node person surrounded in a family in which they do Saturn in a very particular way, for better or worse. And that person can feel he or she can't stand how they do Saturn – what they think an adult is, etc. – and must go do the opposite. Whatever love the family is trying to give might not be recognized or received. It could be that way.

You'll find this in charts and it will be the answer to things like "I can't stop arguing with my parents. They're always criticizing me, never supported me." You look at that and see South Node ruler conjunct the North Node and you can tell them that the soul has set it up so that there wasn't a chance, and let's talk about why instead of just being mad at the family for not being supportive in the right way. Most of our families are supportive it's just that sometimes we can't receive it because the soul's journey says, "Maybe I need to learn through not belonging" or something like this. For me, I need to learn how to belong while creating freedom within family relationships. Do I always do it well? Not always. Often I'm stressed about the conflict I feel. But when I said to my mom that I cannot do that, and she is an adult and loves me and knows I love her, and she can deal with it though it is painful for her. But then that fits with her karmic journey, too: Moon in Aquarius on the 4th house South Node – she learns through family by being at times disconnected, that's one of the ways she learns about family. So we're playing into each others' stories all the time and those family members are cocreating the experience of love not being received by the family member who feels different – there is this whole nexus of souls teaching each other. We didn't get into karma between souls but within families whatever it is that happens in life – just like with an individual soul creating a journey – whatever happens between souls is a co-creation of those souls to learn ,even through pain.

North Node of the Moon

Tom: Using these several steps starting with the Pluto story (what is the soul trying to get done as this person), then the South Node story (what kinds of environments and therefore through what kind of lens does this person choose to see the world), and then the South Node ruler story (what's a person's role in these environments), these three things tell us about the past which tends to be created to be the present. Those three symbols indicate what the person is or might be carrying regarding beliefs. When you're working with your own chart or talking with somebody about his or her chart, all those symbols tell you about where this person has been. Then there is a 4th symbol to look at, the North Node of the Moon, which is where you have not yet been.

Because of the emphasis on choosing certain kinds of families related to the South Node, talking about doing the opposite can be difficult. It can be difficult to want to change – we prefer being comfortable even if it stinks. At least we know about it; we've been there; we know what it is. What happens is that people make up stories about the North Node and what it would be like to do that, including, "I don't want to do that – I don't want to be that kind of person." So we're supposed to grow into it but we're in fact predisposed to not want to do it at all. We will each draw people into our lives who kind of drag us into our North Node. It's a given because we need to grow in that direction so we're vibrating or sending out a broadcast: "Please help me do this." And then we have the choice on how to respond when someone comes in to teach us.

Considering something opposing our habit patterns, it's constant discomfort. Working with clients I can explain to them what the North Node is about and I can contrast it with the South Node, the habit patterns and comfort zone and their default way of doing things. But then they can sit there and nod affirmatively, acknowledging that they understand what I'm telling them, but they might not want to do it. It's a good idea to get down into why they don't want to do it because there tend to be prejudices about becoming this other sort of person. Remember that this person was raised in families in many lives that are represented by the opposite. For me with a Cancer South Node, a focus on emotions and seeing life through an emotional lens. Well, one of the worst things you can do is to only do practical. Tempering it with practical is good but my inner "don't want to change" part will make up all these terrible stories. An example I use frequently is that I would never want to be like people who get up at the same time every day, which might fit with a Capricorn North Node. I would never want to be like those people. But it's not just that – I have a story: "It's so boring. It's so predictable. So routine. What if inspiration strikes in the middle of the night and getting up at 8 a.m. every day doesn't work because this day you need to sleep till noon or you'd ruin the inspiration – why even bother trying to have a pattern if you're just going to—" This whole story and the stupid drama about it. It's just me not wanting to change. I've been conditioned to believe that I live in the sign of Cancer and so when somebody tells me I should get organized and be mature, I dread it. And we do that all the way around the wheel with our South Nodes.

I find it instructive to evaluate people's biases when it comes to the nodes. Automatically I know they prefer the South Node and they probably have prejudices against the North Node. Until we grow up, that is. Some of us have parts that don't really want to change and grow in that direction but it can seem as though parts never grow up that way.

This is the 4th step of this analysis process: What does a person not really know how to do, probably doesn't want to learn how to do, and needs help from others but might not be open to it? The North Node is rounding out the soul's journey. This is what's been left out again and again. I'm always picking families to teach me how to be Cancerian, so Capricorn naturally gets left out.

When I'm listening to clients I'm always listening for those 4 things. I'm hearing what the person tells me whether it's the issue they want to fix or a response to what I've told them with these 4 things in mind:

1. The Pluto thing about what the soul is trying to get done but hurts at the personality level,

2. The South Node thing about what this person thinks the world is about,

3. Who this person thinks he or she is – the South Node ruler stuff – and then

4. What is this person pretty clueless about but could really use understanding about?

When I'm working with people that's what I'm doing, keeping track of all those things. There are key words that jump out like "never," "always," "can't" – those fit somewhere in that 4-step process about their beliefs, which is their karma.

Pluto Generations

Jillian: Pluto represents the soul's deepest intentions and desires, but yet it's a slow mover. Where it is in our charts is different – the houses – but there are Pluto generations. Can you speak to that, the fact that there are soul generations? We understand that there are generational gaps and we're defined by where the planets are, but with Pluto specifically regarding where the soul's desires and intentions are, could you address that?

Tom: This is one of my favorite topics. I love this because it answers so many questions. In *The Soul's Journey I* there's a bit about this but this time here might get into it more deeply.

It is individual. I do not in any way say that the transpersonal planets are impersonal – not at all. Ask a Pisces person if Neptune is impersonal – it rules the Sun. These outer planets affect us personally. With the Pluto generations you have groups of souls that happen to share similar intentions. It's not that they know each other or said, "Oh, yeah! Let's make sure we get in in 1959 all together."

Candace: Are you sure?

Tom: I am.

Candace: I think some of us decided …

Tom: You did? Well, some of you will but it's not that the millions of people will. Because we're talking about Pluto in Leo – the births from around 1938 to 1958, and then 1958 to 1971 with Virgo. It's that they share similar intentions at the soul level. If we talk about two people with Pluto in Virgo in the 8th, I'm going to get generic about each one and then we're going to get specific about each one based in your journey and energy and what you want to know. But you share in common the idea of responsibility within committed, intimate relationship, duty, what belongs to whom/sharing resources – you have that in common and everyone with Pluto in Virgo is working on responsibility.

Candace: Wow.

Tom: I did a version of this one time and someone raised her hand and said, "Some of the biggest slobs I know have Pluto in Virgo." I told her, "Exactly – they're dealing with responsibility … by not doing it, by exploring not having it." So you have these soul groups of people who are incarnating in the same generations to learn lessons at the same time in the same social and historical contexts. Pluto in Virgo people born in the late 1950s and 1960s have a very different experience from those born during the previous time Pluto was in Virgo about 248 years earlier because of the social and historical context.

Michael: The context of the time they come in?

Tom: Yes.

Glenna: Some say Pluto in Virgo is cleaning up the mess of the Pluto in Leo generation.

Tom: Definitely can, yeah. Okay, so let's do this – let's start with Pluto in Cancer. This is what I love about this: tracing history with this. Pluto in Cancer is a bit in 1912, a chunk of 1913, and then enters for good in 1914 until 1937-38. At the soul level they are – actually, let's start with Pluto in Gemini. I'll bet some of your parents have it in Gemini. Let's start with Gemini so you can see some context for Pluto in Cancer.

Gemini

For Pluto in Gemini, the soul-level empowerment comes through curiosity, new information, asking questions, exploring, reaching out, opening up, learning how to be flexible. Take what I'm about to say as applicable to any of the generations. You have these millions of people exploring a theme from different angles but it's the same thing. People who are absolutely closed-minded – Pluto in Gemini. People who are absolutely open-minded – Pluto in Gemini. People who are closed to new information because they don't like what they are finding out – Pluto in Gemini. People who can't stop asking terrific questions – Pluto in Gemini. We don't know a lot of these people now but I wanted to get into this in case your parents were in that generation or you know others in that age bracket so you can understand more about them.

They are empowered when they can get information, answers to questions, data. Disempowered when they can't. In that couple decades of people, and this is applicable to all these generations, exploring the same theme through all these different ways. Coming in with different karmic baggage, assumptions and categories of assumption though they share a lot in common, and biases and prejudices, and fear and pain. For some of these people, the wounding is that they actually got the information they sought and it hurt. Some of the wounding is from not being allowed to ask questions, so the mind is wasted. The wounding can also be never finding the answer, meaning that you have the wrong people to ask. You could have a soul journey of needing to listen to inner guidance so you would attract all kinds of people to you who can't answer your questions. And disempowerment can come through having your voice silenced, or being in a social context in which you can't ask hard questions or speak freely about anything. That's a range of Gemini disempowerment.

Gemini empowerment is obviously the free flow of information, exchange, asking questions, finding people with answers – all that stuff. It's also about perception. The wounding involves lack of clarity about perception because of biases that are shaped by disempowering karmic memories: "I asked you this question and you gave me an answer that sent me down a road that didn't help me. Should I keep asking questions?"

Jillian: *Alice in Wonderland.*

Tom: Really?

Jillian: She gets backwards answers meant to confuse her.

Tom: Oh, right. When was that written?

Jillian: Not sure.

Tom: We're looking it up later. But these people are empowered through getting answers, feeling free to ask questions, and this idea of feeling freedom in picking something up and then dropping it if it doesn't work – Gemini. "Oh, that didn't work. What else? What tools?" Gather, gather, gather. "New tools in my tool box. I only have 21 right now because I live in a small town and I'm uneducated and my parents won't give me money to buy books. Our library is actually in the church basement and has 30 books and 29 of them are about Jesus, and I want to read Darwin." That's a disempowering Pluto-in-Gemini kind of experience. To get empowered sometimes they need to leave the context and go explore, get new data and information. That's the Gemini thing.

Cancer

Archetypally, after you spin out in Gemini, if you don't establish roots and figure out who you really are on the inside, you're lost. Pluto in Cancer comes next. Those people are interested in the nest, security, safety, stability – protection is a giant thing; feeling safe. For some of them it will come out as money and making sure resources are in order but a lot of them it can come out as, "Make sure those people don't come get us." My grandmother had Pluto in Cancer.

Michael: I think my grandmother does, too. They had that sense of having to protect because they were French Jews. They came here with that as their history.

Tom: Exactly! My grandmother had some of that business going on, too. I have this memory which is totally Pluto in Cancer of being in the grocery store with her when I was I think 4 or 5. She's pushing the cart and she has the strap of her purse threaded around her wrist and then she's holding on to the cart –

Candace: I know.

Tom: I told you this story?

Candace: No, I know people like this.

Tom: She's pushing the cart and I'm observing this at eye level because I'm tiny, and sees me looking. She explains why: "That's so the black people don't steal it," referencing the 30-year old woman with her 3- and 5-year old kids across the way. I'm thinking, "They don't want to steal your purse. Look at them – they're just people buying food." That was my grandmother's expression of the fear of the other, which is another thing with Pluto in Cancer because they're trying to establish safety through belonging. The Pluto in Cancer journey involves not belonging, not having cohesion, having societies, nations, families, and clans fall apart in addition to not having food – because food's a marker for love and Pluto in Cancer is trying to figure out where love comes from, this whole generation. Who's supposed to give you love? How do you become empowered through love? How do you become empowered through nurturing? They are seeking to remain inside something, to be safe and protect and to establish walls. Cancer represented by the crab, right, the shell? They are empowered through belonging, connectedness, patriotism, but there's this big thing about Pluto in Cancer with the other. Because if Moon is about belonging these people all have experiences in various lives in which one clan group comes up against another – one ethnic group, etc. – that teaches the soul about connectedness and belonging. "Well, what should I be willing to do when the people with the other skin color are threatening our borders? What should I be willing to do – what's patriotism, what's love of country and clan?"

Leo

Then Pluto in Leo feels that there's more going on than trying to be safe – it's the natural criticism of Leo to Cancer.

Glenna: Stepping out.

Tom: Yeah, I'm setting that up. The Cancer is trying to draw itself in and the Leo says, "Lemme show you who I am! Lemme do my little dance on the table! Let me sing my song!"

Jillian: Let me break out of the house.

Tom: Let me go have fun, let me explore, let me enjoy, let me have opinions that are different than yours.

Jillian: 1938-1957.

Tom: Yeah, maybe '37-38 because there's a little retro dance. So Pluto in Leo is empowered through being recognized as an individual. Consider a group of souls that needs to express themselves individually. [group laughs] Consider millions of people – can you imagine being a school teacher when these kids were 8 years old? Not all of them are boisterous about it because they're dealing with soul wounding of being ignored, too, and treated like a faceless member of a crowd – that's part of the Pluto-in-Leo wounding: *Can't express; nobody's listening; giant tidal wave ruined my chances to become a dancer – why bother being happy?* That's part of this exploration of finding joy because you need to perform the experience of being you, finding the value in individuality. So they are disempowered through being treated like a number, face in the crowd, people can't remember your name.

There's a lot of focus on self here, being empowered through it. It can be easy to traffic in stereotypes in weaker moments or after I've had a couple beers but there's a Leo stereotype of "me me me! It's all about me." Well, the Pluto in Leo generation needs it. At the soul level they need to focus on themselves. Now if they can turn that performance of being the self into something for people – not just serious philosophical value but joy, fun, and play – and they can release others of the expectation of validating them … Because if I want to perform for you I do need validation but it's really good for me in my head to get to the place where it doesn't matter how you react – I just need to show you this thing. I just need you to hear my poem or whatever it is. But disempowered through people ignoring them or not caring about what they say.

Virgo

Now that's all this focus on self and then we move into Virgo. The natural criticism of Virgo to Leo is, "There's more than just you and your ego!" Virgo wants to serve, wants to make something better and seeks in different ways to be selfless even if being an agent of change but trying to be humble about it. Not always succeeding because we're all human, but learning about duty and responsibility over many lives. In Virgo is where we learn about team work and sacrificing egoic interests in the service of making something better. That's where you give up whatever it is to get up every day at 5 a.m. so you can be on that rowing team because you wanted that experience of togetherness.

As part of the Virgo process is making something better part of the wounding is in being unable to meet the responsibilities that are chosen or that are foisted upon one. Another corner of it is from having been burned out from doing too much, the person knows he or she can't complete the task so won't take anything on. But the other part of it is that he or she can see what perfection is – a Plutonian soul-level strength is analysis and categorization to the point where they can see what's imperfect. This is the false dichotomy: "Do I work my butt off to try to make something better even though it's not possible to perfect it or do I throw my hands up in the air and get on the couch and get some bon bons and just waste my life?" And, "Do I submit to pressure or do I refuse to take it on?" Some of the people with Pluto in Virgo are the most stressed out people you will ever meet. Even if a Pluto in Leo person isn't being heard and a Pluto in Cancer person is desperately looking for food, the Pluto in Virgo person is more stressed out because of the pressure, this energy of perfection. But you can't ever do it, you can't get it – it's not possible. It can be a recipe for burnout.

I work with a lot of people who identify as healers. There's a subset of those people – and this is another favorite topic of mine – for whom Chiron or Saturn and Chiron in Pisces oppose Pluto-Uranus in Virgo. It's in the mid-1960s. There's something extremely juicy in there and I worked with a handful of them in the last couple of months and they're judging themselves because they couldn't save enough people, heal enough, and I ask who are they trying to save and why. There's this story about my dad, my mom, my cousin, my daughter. I tell them that each of those people is a powerful, Divine creator and you're not responsible for anything, and they don't get that because somewhere on the Earth time line they have a life in which they're surrounded by people who are suffering and can't help. Either they are handicapped, sick, or dying, or – with some of them when I look into the past-life records I saw a life where they're surrounded by suffering, like they're in a village of 500 people and 300 are sick. Or dying or dead. The people who don't get sick have to rally so they take on a lot of responsibility. But the Chiron in Pisces – the suffering that's out of control, chaos, opposing the Pluto-in-Virgo mission of making something better. You can't save people from the plague if they're dying.

So there's a lot of pressure around that doing. Sometimes I work with people with Pluto in Virgo and I ask what they would be doing if they didn't feel guilty about what they haven't been able to do yet. [group laughs]

Anne: Good question.

Tom: And they say stuff like, "I would work with animals. I would be a painter. I would write novels. I could enjoy something instead of feeling pressed into service."

Jillian: They'd be Pluto in Leo. [group laughs]

Tom: Right! They'd rather do something enjoyable that has an effect instead of just feeling pressure that they can't ever get enough done. A lot of people living that kind of story will manifest some family member they can't save – that kind of thing. So you have people with Pluto here who can't save people. The motivation to be a healer can become pathological if you feel you don't succeed. And sometimes holding someone's hand and lessening suffering as they die is not acceptable when you've set out to heal them. You know what I'm saying?

Group: Wow.

Tom: Because the rest of us might be able to acknowledge how easing suffering during the transition of death could actually be really important but if you set out with a lot of pressure on yourself to help somebody heal and you can't do it, it's 50/50: you might get that you tried and accept it or you might judge yourself for not learning enough, not getting enough sleep, not being smart enough, not having the right tools, etc.

That's Pluto in Virgo – empowered through making something better, service, etc. They're focused on analyzing, categorizing, etc.

Libra

The Libra criticism for Virgo is, "Yeah, but do you ever talk to people? Do you ever find out what people are thinking and feeling? Do you ever let other people hear what you're thinking and feeling?" There's a focus on relationship in Libra. The soul's intention is to learn how to create fairness, harmony, justice, equality, and balance. It does have a lot to do with relationships but it also involves politics and social movements and other things. The wounding is that things are not fair, that there's tyranny, totalitarianism, fascism. The wounding is also that people can't hear you or don't want to, won't listen. Also that you tell people what you want and need and people don't care. "I bring to you what I'm trying to become empowered through and you shut me down."

Jillian: Is that the other, relationships?

Tom: Yes. Then there becomes this inordinate emphasis on the other and defining the self in terms of relationships. *So if you don't like me I don't know how to like myself* – it's part of the blind spot – *and if you love me then I don't have any reason to look at myself because I'm getting the approval I need.* But then if it suddenly goes away and you don't love me then I'm back in the other thing again. Back and forth – the emphasis on the other.

Glenna: As well as the intensity around relationships, sexuality, and homosexuality and all that stuff in that generation.

Tom: Yeah. Empowered through being heard and through listening. We think about humility with Pluto in Virgo but Pluto in Libra requires humility to hear somebody – you really want to say something but you've got to wait because you want to give that other person equal time. You *want* that person to feel heard so you're going to do it.

The wounding can be that there's no fairness, but that can have two threads. One is that *life or the other people are not fair.* The other is that *I'll be damned if I treat anyone else equally because I want what I want.* Libra is not about being nice. It's about learning balance through relationship and that involves being at times the tyrant.

Group: Ohh! What was that?

Tom: One of the routes to learning about that is being unfair, being the agent of a lack of fairness. People talk about Libra and I want to say – actually others have and I haven't heard it in a while so want to do it – that Hitler was a Libra rising – the dude wanted what he wanted. So do we think Libra's nice? I'm a Libra rising – I can be not nice. Libra is not about being nice. Sometimes it's about trying to appear nice so you don't ruffle people and scare them. But some of the wounding with Pluto in Libra is about "I don't like how I treated you." Our mind goes automatically to the victim thing: if a relationship's unfair then we must have gotten the short end of the stick. Well, maybe I'm taking advantage of you and that's part of my wounding. We don't think about this either but when I treat you unfairly, I am affected as well. If I yell at you, hurt you, I'm affected energetically, emotionally, and karmically as well. What we are trying to heal is unfairness of all kinds, all flavors. I wouldn't listen to you or acknowledge your opinion – you told me what you wanted and I didn't value it. Or the other way around. There are just as many people we could classify as perpetrators as victims in relationship with Pluto in Libra – jerks and pushovers are represented in equal numbers and we're all in this generation going back and forth with it.

Scorpio

Next is Pluto in Scorpio. People in that generation have the soul-level intention of being empowered through Scorpio stuff: learning about intensity, power, intimacy, sex – but all of it has to do with becoming empowered through learning about power. When do you take it? When do you give it away? When is the best time to do either? Or is that model inappropriate and needs to be upgraded? All those kinds of questions.

The fears and wounding have to do with being overpowered by others or in making choices that are destructive and overpower self. When you live through the lens of Scorpio there's an intensity you can't help but feel. Think about people you know with Scorpio Suns, Moons, Ascendants, or inner planets but when Pluto is here it's kind of jacked up. Because Pluto, the planet of intensity and learning about life in the deepest way, is in the sign of learning about things in the deepest way.

Some of their fears have to do with giving away too much. That can lead to a resistance to showing who they are, in fact, because knowledge is power. If I reveal to you who I am, what I'm feeling and what I'm really about, you might be able to use that against me later. It doesn't always have to be that you have nefarious motives. It can be that since you know something you can stumble upon my fear button, so I might try to keep myself secret, and what's going on internally. It's not that they are all secretive but there is going to be a line many of them don't cross about revealing the self and being upfront and honest about what's really happening. Scorpio is the sign of feeling very intensely – the water sign with all the depth – so at the soul level they crave depth. They need to reveal who they are on the deepest level and they need to see who other people are on the deepest levels. But building on the intention of the soul we have to understand this layering of strata above that – the debris from experience. As everybody who has anything in Scorpio knows, you reveal something – your truth – and somebody looks at you with disdain or judgment. How does that feel? Not good. These people at the soul level are experiencing that in many, many lives.

The depth of emotions can lead to destructive patterns because if you don't know how to deal with your emotions, your pain, a sense of betrayal and "I'm so intense I can't really show myself to others because it's too much for other people," – that's another thing. Needing the truth, needing exposure and yet believing in some way that it might be too much for others and so it can lead to holding something back. Practically speaking, some of these issues can come out as looking for peak experience. I made a joke last night with somebody here that we're going to get into Pluto in Scorpio in the morning – all about sex, drugs, and rock and roll. There is an intensity of experience that is necessary with this placement and sometimes behaviors and experiences are brought in to intensify life. In this generation there are issues about sexuality as it relates to power, truth, honesty, and revealing the self and seeing others. A lot of them unconsciously will have beliefs – karma – about sex being about power one way or another.

Michael: Like dominating?

Tom: Yes. In the service of learning about the soul-level journey about power through Scorpio they've in different lives dominated and been dominated. These are experiences of power-over and power-under when it comes to anything including sexuality. If you play word-association games with people in different generations you might find people with Pluto in Scorpio holding back a little but if you could read their minds ... you know, there's a lot of what we call darkness that might automatically associate in that way. Not that they're dark

103

people but they've been conditioned in this very deep way by this experience of the heavier, more intense things in life. I had a girlfriend with Pluto in Scorpio and when we started getting to know each other and were talking about this stuff, I was telling her about this soul-level intention of her generation that's happening in the background. She humbly and almost with embarrassment admitted that when she was a kid, the favorite game of her and her playmates was playing rape. Like cops and robbers, cowboys and Indians. There was no rape happening but that kind of drama playing out. I explained to her that all of them were in that same age bracket and were trying to process past-life issues. It can get really intense.

The gift of empowerment is in being honest – if they're willing to. And inspiring other people to be honest, upfront, and real. If they can process their own emotions. If they can learn to heal issues with power-over and power-under. I was talking earlier about a different way of looking at Plutonian empowerment that's about absolute self-knowledge and absolute self-acceptance. If they can get there then that is healing the history of power-over and –under in all arenas of life including sex, drugs, and rock and roll.

The gift is reality. Their criticism to the Pluto-in-Libra generation is, "You are so concerned with what everyone else is thinking about you that you don't even know what's real. You don't know what you'd really say from the bottom of your heart because you're trying to be liked." This is 1984-1995.

It's kind of an interstitial note but when you look at trends that sociologists and psychologists observe – even economists – over time you will see things like suddenly there is this great increase in teen suicide or the prevalence of this or that. Look at when these pieces of information are coming out, when the minds of the scientists are observing the patterns as well as the age of the population they're talking about. Rates of teen suicide in the Pluto in Virgo generation would be one and sexual molestation with kids with Pluto in Scorpio would be another. It's not always true that these things have not been happening already but our consciousness is able to wrap itself around these tragedies that are widespread. And the soul groups are creating certain experiences. We haven't even healed any of the suicide with the Pluto in Virgo generation – not any of it – but it came up for awareness. We still haven't understood – we have no idea what to do with suicide, anyway, which is another 2-day workshop. [group laughs]

So that's the Scorpio thing – empowered through truth but terrified of being overpowered or overpowering others. One more note about that. There's this thing when you're dealing with Scorpionic people – you can tell where they are by how much eye contact they can make with you. If they're in a healthier place they can stay with you until you need to disengage for a bit. But there's this intensity that comes even just through the eyes because eye contact opens the door to emotional connection. You may find people with Pluto in Scorpio need contact but they might not always be clear about the best way to create it.

That's the Scorpio thing – lots of drama.

Sagittarius

Then Sagittarius comes along. The natural criticism of Sagittarius to Scorpio is, "You don't have any clue about what's important because you're just cycling through this drama with sex, drugs, and rock and roll. You're so wrapped up in your emotions and bogged down in creating drama where there might not even be any that you can't even have joy or see the big picture." The group with Pluto here is at the soul level intending to have faith, hope, optimism – to have something to believe in. They are empowered through believing in something which often – because of the disempowering Plutonian experiences over many lives – can only come through looking at the disillusionment and processing it, and then choosing to believe in something again. They need to believe but many of them will be sardonic, sarcastic, unable to believe in good things, jaded, disillusioned. Growing up within religious structures but feeling bereft, empty, with a dearth of meaning while perhaps surrounded by people who are saying, "God said this and everything's great!" And these people will feel, "How can you possibly believe that?" But they grow up in that. Or they can jump in wholeheartedly because that's the passion at the soul level, the conviction, that comes with Pluto here. Religion is a vehicle for the experience of meaning and the search for truth. Not all of them are going to be religious, obviously, but they are going to be dealing with issue about belief. They will have issues about empowerment through the function of higher mind. Some of these people have disempowered educational experiences. Many of them will have incredibly strong imaginations that they might want to limit so that they don't get themselves in further trouble like in some lives. But the imaginative power – the power of the gods can come through these people in the form of imagination, the right brain, the ability to envision something and hold it in the mind and then be able to create it. We create our realities through our beliefs and if you hold a belief in a certain way you create reality around you. These people become empowered through that process of holding a vision and making it real.

Some of the experiences in various lives that have left them disempowered and disillusioned have to do with doing that and then finding out a truth that reveals what they were believing in to be false. That can be within religion when working with doctrine and then personally experiencing some higher truth, some bit of natural law that ruined the belief. You can be living this way for decades, raising your family this way, and then you find out it's not true. The rug can be pulled out from under your capacity to believe.

Michael: Could those people be inclined to think they have all the answers? I have friends who are Sagittarius who are so strong in what they believe – "we are the ones you should follow."

Tom: Yes. That is one of the things that can come with this placement. Fitting with that, they need to believe – to have something to believe in – but they can get so fixed that they can't take in new information, listen to other people, and get new ideas. They can get stale and stuck. Sagittarius is the archer and it's not about drawing the bow but about what happens when you release the bow – it's gone, it's in flight. The arrow has its own momentum. The truth about Sagittarius energy is that you need to believe something but you can change your mind halfway through and upgrade your belief. Or switch it. But people who are living Sagittarius stories don't want to know that because it seems it might cheapen everything they are experiencing.

Michael: Makes it flakey.

Tom: Exactly. There are people who live this energy strongly who do change their minds and seem flakey. You might not look at him and think he's a Sagittarian figure but Noam Chomsky, the linguist, has done this. He laid out his thoughts and was clear. People make their minds do acrobatics to be able to digest what he's saying – he's a philosopher, a linguist. But he's working with a belief. He laid out his philosophy and others took to it. Years later he changed his mind about pretty much all of that first statement. Then he put out a book stating where he was after reconsidering his original theses and then everyone who had followed the original system of thought he'd laid out years earlier had to adapt to this new view. And they follow it – they take it in and decide that he's right to change his mind. And then years later he says he's heading

108

in a different direction and there are people who are with him and there are people who are frustrated and there are others who begin to hate him as a result of his change of mind. But he's a Sagittarian figure. He's like, "Here's the truth – I'm sure. It's true." And then he lets himself change his mind when it seems that he should.

Michael: He was influential in many education circles, and no one wanted to change that base. I saw that. We didn't want that to change – that was our base.

Tom: *You just gave us a piece of the truth and now you're going back on it?* And he's like, "Well, it no longer seems to work." That's a good model for all of us who run Sagittarian energy. Personally, I have Moon-Mercury-Neptune there. I take that model and there are things I change my mind about. For instance in *The Soul's Journey I* Pluto is step number 3 in the 4-step process and now I use it as number 1 – it seems to work better. [group laughs] It feels better. So we need to believe something but the risk is in becoming dogmatic and inflexible – that's the point.

Annette: My ex was Gnostic, I was exploring Islam, my daughter was a Buddhist at the time, and my son was a Christian. We were all living in the same home.

Tom: Did you all have specialized diets? Like four different dinners – I can eat meat but only this kind? [group laughs]

Annette: This was after they went through many religions with me and decided to have their own.

Tom: With Pluto in Sagittarius, they need to believe something and be one-directional and one of the blind spots is being too one-directional and not being flexible with reality. Humans have a natural need to believe something and to seek meaning and these people are majoring in it at the soul level. But there's been a lot of disillusionment and disempowerment through beliefs, whether through being too fixed and dogmatic or believing in something that turned out not to be true. These are the births from 1995-2007, so they're young – the oldest is 16. If they can understand this basic truth that humans need to have, seek, and create meaning but that we also evolve over time and so what we plug into that meaning port can change, then they'll be able to heal a lot of the stuff that they've been carrying around for many lives. Again, some of it will happen through religion, some through the refusal of religion – the on-going theist-atheist debate that's always going down on Earth. But it is all about belief and being able to hold a vision in the mind.

Capricorn

Then we have Capricorn, and the oldest of those with Pluto in Capricorn is 3 years old. The natural criticism of Capricorn to Sagittarius is, "You're so focused on what you would like to be true that you can't just get off your butt and make something happen. You're so dreamy and imaginative – so living in the world of imagination – that you choose not to accomplish something. You never make anything of lasting value." It's a criticism about tangibles versus intangibles because Sagittarius is focused on creating tangibles out of intangibles – creating the world in terms of belief – but Capricorn needs to create the world with the hands and because of reality and necessity.

These people have the soul-level intention of becoming empowered through constructing and building real structures, long-term projects, through achieving real-world goals, and working hard at things. It's going to be interesting to watch these little babies grow into toddlers and then older children – including many children who haven't even been born yet because this is there until 2024. What they really need is to do something substantial in a concrete way. They need to become empowered through building something, becoming mature, becoming competent, through doing something well and being recognized for doing it well. That's a huge thing for them. The wounding is being blocked from accomplishment, seeming to fail at achieving something, and issues with ambition, too. We can look at many individual journeys with Pluto in Capricorn needing to become empowered through developing and acting on ambition. So the karmic wounding can involve not acting on it, being blocked from acting on it, or not putting a plan in place.

We talked earlier about Pluto in Virgo and the kind of criticism they can carry. They can see perfection and might not be able to make it happen, resulting in karmic histories of attempting to make something better but maybe not achieving it all the time. The Pluto in Capricorn people – babies – will have a similar kind of thing because of the expectations they have on themselves to be respected, good at something, and then recognized for being good at it.

Because they are learning about power through dealing with authority figures – ultimately the goal is that they become authority figures – they will manifest authority figures who block them at least part of the time. Because they are learning about becoming empowered with Saturnian, Capricorn figures some of these kids will be born to parents who are big energetically and perhaps harsh. Not necessarily abusive but there are going to be very distinct elder-younger roles. These kids have questions at the soul level about what it takes to be authoritative, what does it require to be respected, what age means, etc. They might naturally be inclined to respect people who are older so they are also going to draw older people who are like kids, who can't teach them anything, or can't take responsibility for themselves or others. You can see that because they need to be respected they will draw teachers to them who might not be. We can know that for sure because of the nature of learning as a human – we often draw to us the opposite of what we need to become.

Glenna: The thing I notice about my 3-year old grandson is that he will say, "Hi Granny, how was your day? Did you work hard today?" It's about work. [group laughs] He's an old soul already – you can see that it in his eyes. And he's valuing work.

Candace: Here's another one: My son and his wife have a 2-year old. He was born on the Full Moon with Moon on

Pluto. Her parents are like the kids that she's drawn as the teachers but in reality she's running the show. And I can see it.

Tom: Exactly.

Candace: I think it's going to be very interesting.

Tom: Yeah!

Glenna: They're little elders.

Tom: Sometimes it will come as power struggles but sometimes it'll just be the reversal of the young one teaching and controlling, and then how that kid is going to grow up to be an authority figure having been in that dynamic as a kid – lots of soul growth possible being the youngest generation in a family.

Respect and autonomy are giant for this generation. Part of the wounding can be that they didn't get elbow room to work on their long-term projects and goals. So you'll find some with family karma of being one of 11 kids on a farm hundreds of years ago where you can't work on something until you're an adult but there might be a kid with a vision of some project – even an invention. If they can take models of authority that they are presented with and be forgiving with them, like, "This is how my parents are raising me and wow, that is dumb, and that's stupid, and they shouldn't do it that way" – if they can take the models they are presented with as learning opportunities but be compassionate about it, that will be hard for many of them but good. It would be hard because they have judgments about how things are supposed to go. And assuming that they are the final authority. They'll be really

113

good at certain things so they'll feel authoritative but they'll be 7 years old. [group laughs] And not understanding anything else but the thing that they're good at. That will be interesting to watch unfold.

I talked with Michael yesterday after we did the first few signs about tying it to history. You can look at the history any country, social movements, political change, economic unfolding, based in the decisions individuals are making. Again, two things: the time in which they are making those decision and then how they are wired natally. What age group is doing this? Also keep in mind the natural criticism that each has of the others. Signs that are next to each other will have an automatic natural criticism. Signs that are two away will be sextile – they might not have a criticism. They might be a little more supportive but they do have input. So you might look at how Libra might offer constructive feedback to Leo or Scorpio to Virgo or Virgo to Cancer. You can look at those relationships. You can look at a person with Pluto in Scorpio who has a grandparent with Pluto in Leo – a natural square. They might automatically get long, love each other, and be supportive but they have some criticisms for each other. Usually we hear the criticisms of older people to younger people because we're accustomed to being concerned about how we're raising our people but it also goes the other way. Candace, your kids were talking to you about something today. They were looking at your Leo and wanting to help you with it – it's the same thing. They're Pluto in Libra sextiling your Leo.

I'm interested in family dynamics and generational dynamics we are fundamentally wired in different ways from each other. When I'm clear I'm really good at Libra, and when you're clear, Candace, you're really good at Leo and Glenna, when you're clear you're really good at Virgo. We have different ways of doing things and all are valuable. And when I say "really good at" I mean that the most empowered thing you could possibly do is that. Your soul is saying, "I need to become expert because my emotional health rests on doing life through this lens well."

Example Charts

Annette

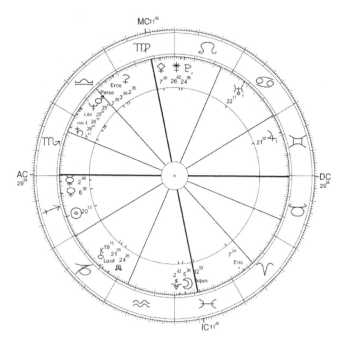

December 12, 1953, 5:28 AM

Tom: Annette, How do you feel about going first?

Annette: Go for it.

Tom: I want to start with this first chart in a general sense using the four steps we talked about this morning. Then we will get into karma and beliefs and actually talking with Annette but I want to run you through it.

Starting with Annette's Pluto in Leo in the 9th house. Her soul's intention involves to be empowered through expressing (Leo) belief (9th house). Leo's about creative self-expression, being recognized as an individual, and sharing the self in – I think of it as being in a performative way. It's not simply me telling you who I am but I think of it as performing the experience of being me. That's where we get creative stuff that takes us into art, drama, dance, and music and that kind of creativity. It's really about creative expression: who are you as an individual?

A lot of Annette's multilife journey has to do with working within 9th-house – which is to say belief, religious, educational contexts – and being seen as an individual and having her individual voice honored. When we talk about empowering and disempowering experiences, Pluto in the 9th is a classic setup for being born into a very religious family or a very philosophically-oriented family and not feeling that individual voice honored at all because the empowerment journey requires figuring out how to do that. The family of origin might be teachers in the form of not honoring the individual voice.

Pluto is also retrograde, which means that things have to work differently. We can probably safely assume in Annette's family whoever is religious or anti-religious is very serious about it but the way they think about it could never work for her. She's got to redo it, she's got to reinvent the wheel of belief in these lives. We get Pluto retrograde in the chart when we adopt other people's models of how to do things when it comes to Pluto. We might think, "Well, these other people are kneeling and talking about this thing for God so I think that's what prayer must be like so I'm going to do that." And then you're doing it and you think, "I don't really think this is very interesting at all. I don't even know why I'm doing this." But other people were doing it so you modeled it.

Annette: A lot of people don't know this about me. I was a childhood minister probably at 11 years old. Prophesying and doing the whole bit.

Tom: Karmic repeat – repeating what you sow.

Annette: Like Oral Roberts and the tent thing.

Tom: So you ran with it, and then what happened?

Annette: I matured really early, quick, and fast. Divorced around 27 and began studying metaphysics and Eastern religions.

Tom: Okay. Pluto in the 9th is a classic signature of being born into religion and having it eventually not work for you.

Annette: My father was a minister, my dad's sister owns a church, my husband was a minister.

Tom: I'll just tell you regarding this idea of empowerment and disempowerment in different lives, in some lives you have this thing where you want to divorce it but you don't, and you just do it. Because you're committed.

Annette: That's what I did.

Tom: When did you want to stop? You said you stopped it around age 27 but when did you want to?

Annette: Earlier than that.

Tom: Think about that period from when you realized you didn't want to do it and when you actually stopped doing it. That period is the fork-in-the-road opportunity for karmic growth. In some lives you just do the religion thing because that's what you're doing and then at the end of your life you're like, "oh, I wish I would have read more books."

Annette: I was really upset when I figured out driving home one night from work that [inaudible] and I was pretty pissed off.

Tom: Some people in that situation would not have continued studying metaphysics but been disillusioned. You have that karma, too.

Annette: I've been disillusioned.

Tom: But not enough to not come out of it. Some people don't come out of it.

Annette: The only way I came out of it was that I had 3 deaths. My mother died, a baby died, and my best friend died all in October one year right after the other around age 27. So I began to question when this whole inner [inaudible]. My best friend died first and then I had a child. I knew as soon as the baby was born that she wasn't going to live. So I was questioning things then, and struggling with if I had an abortion and were to have another child born with this defect. It just shook my whole religious – it shook everything, my faith, my belief system, and everything. It had to do with realizing suddenly that other people think differently about what happens with life after death. That started me on my journey of exploring.

119

Tom: And recovering the ability to have faith in something outside a religious context –

Annette: But then when I started Buddhism I became disillusioned with it for the very simple fact that it left me hopeless. Once you get off that wheel of karma and you know that you're completely responsible for everything that you draw in your life, everything you bring in your life, you can't change it – why be here? And it did not empower me to change.

Tom: You're giving us different explanations of the up and down, on and off, yes or no, go or stop – that's what I want to point out to you. Empowered, disempowered. Believing, disillusioned. That's the karmic cycle for you regarding the Pluto. So your soul is learning about the ability to have faith and belief.

Annette: In myself.

Tom: Well, that's your evolution. That's where you ultimately get after being a minister of someone else's words and ideas, and then studying ancient traditions that are different, and it's all disillusionment until you can have faith in something that's a constant, which is your own psyche, being, etc. So that's your roller coaster. We're all doing a roller coaster with Pluto: empowerment, disempowerment. But I'll tell you, this stuff about evolution of consciousness, 2012, and the Mayan Calendar and the veils between dimensions dissolving including the partitions in our own consciousness that keep past lives out of awareness – most of us in this life are having a lot more roller coasters than we would in any other given life. Now you're able to integrate more so you're experiencing more of the ups and downs on steeper grades.

I said to you that there are some lives in which you don't stop the preaching even when you're done and you're hardened, yet now you have the roller coasters of a bunch of different lives happening now in this life. It's to give you the opportunity to re-experience things so that you can change your mind about beliefs. Repeating things but getting to choose different outcomes. It's the same thing in this life with relationships. In another life you meet somebody when you're 15 and you marry when you're 16 and –

Annette: That's what happened in this life!

Tom: Wow! And in another life that partner was your partner for 50 years and in this life less. Some people might feel crappy about themselves if they've been married 4 times but you know what? Things really are sped up and many lives need to get accounted for now. Life-long partnerships serve some but other people are doing 5 years here, 10 years there, 25 years there. It's not quite the same thing as in other lives. So much more has to get fit in in this life.

That's the basic story on your Pluto in the 9th. It's also conjunct the asteroid Juno, which is a soul-level commitment to finding the right way to believe. When you do figure out what works for you you're going to be committed to it, which actually heightens the potential for disillusionment but it also heightens the strength of conviction when you find the right thing.

Pluto is square the Ascendant and Mercury. Mercury's in the 1st – it's a Scorpio Ascendant but Mercury's in Sagittarius and conjunct Venus. On the personality level she carries a lot of communication energy – student, teacher, writer, communicator – all of that. But karmically she is squared by Mercury and it will bring up issues when she wants to write and communicate. Her soul's mission – what her soul is trying to get done – is squared by communicators. And they're in Sagittarius so they probably believe things strongly. They're in the 1st house, so they're probably pretty bold, perhaps brash. You'll naturally attract these people. They're going to be your family members, too, and a lot of other people in your life. But you're naturally going to attract Mercurial people who are fixed in their beliefs who square you, who bring you friction. The soul is asking to learn about right communication through being pressured by communicators. And it's all about belief – they believe, you believe. That's the Pluto setup for you, the whole kit-and-caboodle at the soul level.

The South Node for you is in Cancer in the 8th house[11] and it's conjunct Uranus and opposing a couple of things we'll talk about. The South Node in the 8th house says her soul keeps picking families where there's an emphasis on 8th-house stuff: what we share with others, emotional dynamics that are pretty intense and deep, intimacy, sexuality – this is where things get tangled up with other

[11] The charts in this book depict the North Node of the Moon. The South Node is always exactly opposite.

people whether it's finances, emotions, or sexuality. This is happening through the lens of Cancer so there's a strong emphasis on family, connectedness, emotions, history, who we are in terms of the people we come from, lineage issues. And then Uranus is there, so these families are saturated – that's a key word for a planet conjunct the South Node – with Uranus. But it's in Cancer and it's retrograde so it works a little differently. When Uranus is on the South Node the family has experienced sudden change, which could be innovation, trauma, or both.

So, Annette, you're born into a family that's carrying 8th-house emotional trauma. There are going to be things passed down energetically through your family that have nothing to do with anybody who's doing the passing down. You can intuit, "Mom treats me this way because her mom treated her that way because her family treated her that way." That kind of thing. But there's some kind of original trauma – Uranus in Cancer on the 8th-house South Node – that the family carries and passes down through generations. Whether or not that emphasis on religion helps heal it or keep it away from it, there's some kind of trauma that defines the family system is what I'm getting at.

Personality-wise you come in very aware of Uranus, which is sudden change.

Annette: I expect it.

Tom: That's the karma.

Candace: It's what's comfortable.

Annette: Pretty much.

Tom: Waiting for something crappy to happen?

Annette: Not as much lately.

Tom: Sure, you change.

Annette: I don't define myself by it anymore. Usually there's some hidden information that can really surprise.

Tom: That's part of it. So that's the South Node. Part of her will be habituated to live in the 8th house through an emotional lens and to expect something quick or traumatic to happen. Now let's talk about the squares to the nodes. They are Mars, Neptune, and the true Black Moon Lilith. How many of you are familiar with the true Black Moon? Not many? Okay, then I'll tell you about it because it will tell us some important things about Annette's story.

Lilith represents our connection to the internal and the external wild. There's a lower-chakra instinct that comes in when it comes to Lilith.

Annette: That was the hardest thing for me to discern for a long time, the difference between instinctual and actual. So you're saying that Lilith is more connected …

Tom: Can we tap into the wisdom of the Earth? Can we recognize the wisdom in the cycles of nature? When it's time to eat something, how do you choose what you eat? Does your body speak to you or is it your brain saying, "Well, this is what I brought" or "this is what's available"? When Lilith is healthy we're in touch with our bodies as far as food, exercise, sleep, nutrition, sexuality – the wisdom of the –

Annette: That's where I'm going.

Tom: Here it's with Mars and Neptune in Libra and square the nodes. Squares to the nodes have to do with unresolved issues wherein people know something about it but not enough to stop tripping over their own shoe laces. For you, Mars-Neptune-Lilith. Mars is assertion and will. Neptune here is aligning that assertion and will with higher truth. And then Lilith – instinct. You already know a lot about it but it probably keeps getting you into trouble. In Libra, it's happening within relationships. Truth in relationships.

Annette: Yeah, yeah. It gets me – I'm learning to separate. So that my experience is my own experience and theirs is theirs.

Tom: Perfect. Look at the course of your learning about it over this life. It is a microcosm of your whole soul's journey of trying to learn that.

When we have squares to the nodes we make assumptions because we have these habits. We find ourselves doing this and that over and over again while getting the same result, and it stinks, and we wonder why it's a problem. We don't see that we can do something in a new way. We have to look at our assumptions and habit patterns and then choose to do something new. Squares to the nodes are life-long learning opportunities. We can learn new things but we also have to give up the identity of someone who does it in a certain way. For example, with Mars-Neptune-Lilith, equality in relationship. Eventually in your adult life you will learn if not already that when a relationship is getting started, you have to tell the other person who you are. But you have to take time to figure that out first and then be clear about it. Think about relationships you had as a teenager – you got married at 16 and that didn't happen then. You just got married and you did what people do when they get married, which often isn't sitting down and having a heart-to-heart on "who I really am." So you learned eventually through the difficult experience, "Oh! *That's* how it has to work."

Conjunct the North Node is the same as opposite the South Node, which means it's as far away as possible from where we came from. So her people live in the 8th house in Cancer. They can't teach her what's on the North Node in Capricorn – they don't know how to do it and therefore can't teach her. Her North Node is in Capricorn in the 2nd house and it's conjunct Chiron and the asteroid Lucifer.

I'll say a little about Lucifer. It is our capacity to believe in ourselves and then bring light but it comes out as the voice of doubt because we don't want to do something selfish and be arrogant. This Cancer South Node wants to see everything through the feeling of it. The Capricorn North Node says you are to be realistic. South Node in the 8th represents sharing with others, defining yourself in terms of your relationships. The North Node in the 2nd is about who you are, what you need, and who you really are as an individual. The Capricorn/2nd North Node is about the invitation and challenge to grow into being realistic about what is self-worth, why you should have it, who deserves to create it, and where it comes from. It's realism.

A kind of rolling up sleeves and getting your nose on the grindstone, practical – doing things to create self-worth.

Chiron there means that this hypersensitivity is about her self-worth, to her capacity to become somebody who is respected. Lucifer's there so there's this element of the voice of doubt: *If I really do that, people will call me arrogant.* The learning becomes being willing to trust your heart and the fact that how other people react to you is not about you.

That's the nodal setup for Annette. She comes in saturated with Uranus because that's on the South Node. She comes in with a certain amount of knowledge but also some blind spots about Mars-Neptune-Lilith because they're square the nodes. And then she comes in needing start from scratch with this Chiron-Lucifer conjunct the North Node.

As our first example, she happens to have this loaded nodal structure. Some people don't have anything in these positions. Lots of people do but some people don't. What we just talked about has a lot to do with her family, too. We know that her parents, grandparents, and siblings if she has any are going to have some degree of need to learn about expression of will and aligning will to higher truth. They're going to need to come out of trauma, whatever that trauma might be. And they're going to need to experience their own self-worth outside their relationships. The nodal structure tells us about her but it also tells us about her family group and some things that they have in common. Not that everybody in the family has the same nodal structure or symbols, but their experiences as souls will resonate with this. We will however find Uranian-Cancerian signatures in your family. You might have family members with Uranus in the 4th house or Uranus on the South Node, too – it's going to be a theme in the family system because it is conjunct the South Node. The symbols might be different. That's the second step of the analysis.

The third step is the South Node ruler by sign. The South Node is in Cancer so we go to the Moon, which is in the 3rd house in Pisces conjunct Vesta. Vesta's an asteroid that has to do with taking something very, very seriously to the point of religious dedication. I call it "religiosity." So she's coming from this Cancerian 8th-house place and she herself is Piscean-3rd house and takes it very seriously. Her voice and mind, what she has to say she takes seriously. We don't look at her as a Moon figure but as defined by the conjunction to the South Node ruler.

There's a resonance here between emotional and energetic sensitivity that your people have – South Node in the 8th in Cancer – and you as the South Node ruler in Pisces in the 3rd house: being aware of things. But you are probably more capable of thinking through things and communicating about what you're feeling than the people you come from. That's where we can see a little difference between the South Node ruler being in the house of communication versus the South Node in the house of "we are entangled." It's hard to think straight sometimes when you live in the 8th house because you're wrapped up, entangled.

This Moon is square Mercury-Venus in the 1st house as well. Earlier I said that Pluto being squared by this Mercury says that her soul's mission receives friction from bold communicators who believe things very strongly. So she will manifest religious figures, even in a life where there's no religion – there'll be philosophers and it'll be the exact same thing. Or they'll be culture shapers or politicians – exact same thing. Separately, on another level, she individually will feel squared by them, too, because her role in these various lives is being squared by the Mercury-Venus. So this Mercurial energy and friction is coming from all sides. It seems to me like this is a soul's intention about getting to the place where you're actually, really, truly thinking straight. You're getting Mercury friction from all over the place. Some people come in to develop ideas but your thing about communication is being in this world surrounded by all this stuff about belief and sorting through it and getting intentional, and then whatever comes later will come – because you are a writer, right? If you haven't already, you are.

Annette: Yes.

Tom: This communication faculty within you has the need first to get straight.

Annette: I find myself thinking, "Can you tell me anything I haven't heard before? Something you can challenge me on? It's all boring."

Tom: Well, that leads you to be a generator of communication. Ultimately, if you get bored like that then you have to share what you want to hear. But in the mean time I understand getting frustrated with what you are hearing.

When I sit down with a chart before I see a client, I take a piece of paper and I'll do that whole analysis in symbolic short hand. I'll write the glyphs for Pluto in Leo in the 9th, and then a square and the glyphs for Mercury-Venus and so on. I do that to get the story in my mind, though it might not work for everybody. And then I when I'm talking to the person I have the sheet filled with the symbols and their relationships next to the chart and I can refer back.

Annette: So you just picked up my themes?

Tom: Yeah. Because before I talk to you I don't know how it manifests. You could be born in a family of atheists. With this setup in the 9th house and this Sagittarius stuff it could actually end up not being about religion.

Annette: It's not.

Tom: You're seeing through it. But what I mean is that a person born a block away five minutes later could have almost the same chart and be born into a family of atheists, which is still about belief but nothing to do with religion. Or people who think that if you don't have your Ph.D. then you might as well jump off a bridge – you know, with the higher education side of the 9th house. There are a lot of people who have charts like there where it's not about religion at all even though once you live it you know it's

130

not about religion, but religion for many others with this setup might never come into the picture.

Annette: It's about the information. I couldn't go to the university so that's where I got my information.

Tom: Higher truth. Honestly, that's an arc that a lot of humans live through.

Annette: I studied Islam, I studied Hinduism – I don't think there's a religion I haven't studied at one time or other. And I moved through them very fast, always with a period of about three years. With some of them I knew that in three years I was going to get bored and move on but with some of them I didn't know what it was going to be. Some of them I got stuck in just a little bit longer but basically in and out within three to four years.

Tom: Two things. One is that you need routes to find truth and religions are a great way to look for that, very common and prevalent. A structure where people have figured out a whole cosmology or something. The other thing is that you're cycling through different lives in which – you might in some life be stuck in Catholicism and you might have heard about these other people, Muslims, and you're curious and have a hankering to find out about that. In this life you move from thing to thing.

People who have religious karma don't ever do just one religion over the course of many lives because in this one life you're in China 3,000 years ago and in this other one you're in the middle of Saudi Arabia in some other part of the time line. People who have 9th-house karma will have cycled through bunches of religions. Like I said, in this life, having a lot of lifetimes and qualities of experience from different lifetimes compressed into one life – three years per religion; you've got a limit.

Annette: I say that this is the best.

Tom: Good! We're glad you're here. Because we're the only truth, really. [group laughs]

Annette: I found it again, didn't I?!

Tom: So that's how I look through the chart.

Jillian: I'm curious because you went to the Mars-Neptune-Lilith that square the nodes, and you mentioned it was in Libra and about relationships. I was going to ask you if you could address the 11th house issue but also something else. I know you have your 4-step process which ends with the North Node but when you have a square to the nodes do you add that in sort of as a final step? Like Steven Forrest would view that as a skipped step[12] and a lot of people believe that the tension in the T-square is resolved through the Mars-Neptune-Lilith in Libra. Do you add that on as a kind of focus to resolve the tension in order to get to the North Node?

Tom: In a way yeah, because you can't get to the North Node if you don't stop tripping over your shoe laces, but I don't end the story there. I do that in the middle of the nodal stuff because I point out this habit pattern, that you have certain assumptions about how you should respond to these things and it's just not enough. But I don't end the story there. I don't like "skipped step" – I really just

---

[12] Steve Forrest seems to prefer the term "missed step" while "skipped step" appears in the work of Jeff Green.

fundamentally don't believe in that because it's an unresolved issue, is how I think of it. You know many things about it, just not enough to feel successful or happy. You do know about it. Annette knows how to have relationships where she doesn't tell the truth. She knows how not to reveal herself. She knows how to hide the Lilith-Mars – she knows how not to speak up for herself. She also knows how to abuse other people if she wants.

Jillian: Where are you getting that from?

Tom: Mars-Lilith square the nodes in Libra. Mars square the nodes is experiencing violence from both angles.

Jillian: And the 11th house?

Tom: It's about where all this is headed. The relationship patterns would not serve where she wants her life to be in 20 years – by default. And then she can choose to be forward-looking and think about where she wants this to go.

The thing with the squares to the nodes is … there are different opinions and I might have heard them all as I tried to figure out my own way of doing it. I started looking at mine and I have 6 squares to the nodes including the Ascendant-Descendant axis. I realized that I know a ton about it but I just keep shooting myself in the foot with it. I really do know about it. Venus in Libra – I can do that. I just do it in a way that leaves me feeling messed up later so I have to learn to make new choices.

Annette: That's my will.

Tom: Yes. And there will be a lot of tension in there but only when things come up. You can spend a long time avoiding having to make a decision about a square to the nodes because you know that you keep messing it up – it doesn't go right or work well. You know how if every time when you were 8 you set the dinner table you put the fork in the place where your parents didn't want you to and they kept telling you? Part of you might say, "Well, then I just shouldn't do this anymore."

Jillian: I noticed that Arjunsuri[13] is also with that Pisces Moon.

Tom: Yeah, let's do that. Arjunsuri is an asteroid whose interpretation I've introduced. It's about where we get answers to the most important questions. The story has to do with Arjuna in the *Bhagavad Gita*. Arjuna's a warrior and he goes on the battlefield and he's supposed to enter into battle with his family because there's a tension and they had tried diplomatic means, tried to be reasonable, and now they have to go to war. He stops at the edge of the battlefield and he sees his cousins, tutors, uncles, and whatnot and he just can't do it. He can't kill his family – he feels it's wrong. His charioteer, who is supposedly a servant, is actually Krishna in disguise – God – and reveals himself to Arjuna and tells him to do it. They have a philosophical discussion at the edge of the battlefield, outside time (because Krishna can do that because he's God), and Krishna tells him that this is his job because Arjuna is a warrior – a member of the warrior caste. Krishna explains that given the events that lead to this

---

[13] Asteroid 20300, explained in detail in *Living Myth: Exploring Archetypal Journeys*.

134

situation, Arjuna is justified in doing this and that he in fact has to do it. He reveals his awe-inspiring splendor to make the point that he is God. Arjuna is wowed by the display and recognizes Krishna as God. But going to battle with his family still doesn't feel right to him. God is telling him to do it and he still doesn't feel right about it. They have an extended conversation until Arjuna's ready to begin the battle.

An authority figure says, "Do this!" and if your conscience says, "Yeah, I don't think I can," then it's an Arjunsuri story. Annette's coming from this 8th-house Cancerian karma – wrapped up with the family – and the 9th house Pluto – a long and intense journey to do with belief, etc. – and then this asteroid conjunct the South Node ruler: she's seeking to listen to the inner voice without sacrificing connection, family, safety, security, survival, etc.

Annette: Exactly.

Tom: It comes down to how big of a big deal for you conscience and inner wisdom are. If God says, "Treat people this way!" and you know you can't do that, God will keep saying it and you have to take back the power and not do it. That's the Arjunsuri bit of her story.

Jillian: Thank you.

Tom: You're welcome. Do you see how that 4-step method comes in? I just go one by one: what does she think life is about?, etc.

Annette: You're reading my personality and character.

Tom: I'm telling you what your soul is trying to get done and all the debris that's been accumulating as a result of the choices. While lots of details get added, for me the 4-step process also points out how any chart reveals how we are each the same. The complexity of each of us is structured the same way: *my soul has a mission like yours does, I keep picking families that have similar themes just as you do, I have a role in those environments and I have a subidentity just like you, and there's something I don't really know how to do and I need people to teach me.* It's exactly the same for every single human. The process of analysis allows us to get complex while honoring how each person is different, too.

I'm glad that speaks to you. With people who have been doing astrology for quite a while and then they read *The Soul's Journey I* or take classes with me—

Annette: I'm sitting here thinking, "Gee, I'm glad I have that book."

Tom: I hear it quite a bit. People tell me that they've been doing this a long time but that this method adds a new angle that really works well for them.

Candace

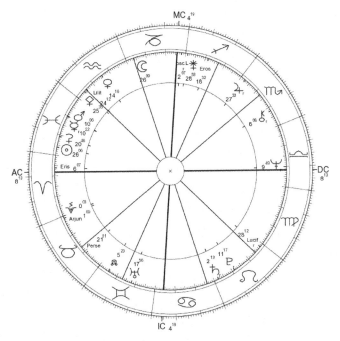

March 17, 1947, 6:55 AM, Chariton, IA

Tom: So let's go to Candace's chart next. First we go to Pluto in Leo in the 5th. The soul intends to become empowered as Candace through self-expression, being recognized as an individual, and performing the experience of being her. It's conjunct Saturn and they are each retrograde. The conjunction is 9 degrees and I count that with Pluto and the nodes. Also I feel that when I talk to her. Pluto conjunct Saturn says that the soul needs to learn about empowerment through becoming Saturnian, which would be authoritative, competent, mature, respectable, moral, and ethical. That both are retrograde says that she's going to be surrounded by people who do those things – self-expression, maturity, morality, and ethics – in ways that don't work for her. She has to invent her own Pluto-Saturn wheel. It's a guaranteed setup to have to do your homework and start looking around and saying, "That doesn't work for me." Most people with these kinds of retrogrades, by the way, get to a place that could last for years where they say, "Oh, well I guess there's nothing worth doing in that after all," because they don't realize they're supposed to make up their own way of doing it.

Candace: Waiting for the other.

Tom: Which we all do naturally. When we're little kids someone might come to us and say, "Let me show you how to grease that bicycle chain." Then we're a little older and someone says, "Let me show you how to write a 5-paragraph essay." Then older and someone says, "Let me show you how to drive." And then later we're looking for people to help us learn how to do things – we naturally do that. We grow up but we have also taken so much instruction that it's natural. But with retrogrades, especially two outer planet retrogrades like this, you're supposed to invent the wheel of self-expression.

Annette: Can you say that again?

Tom: She has to invent her own wheel regarding self-expression. I often say "reinvent the wheel" but it's really about inventing her own way of doing it.

Annette: Because it's retrograde?

Tom: Yes. We'd look at it in regular astrology and say that the energy's turned inward. What that means functionally is that every manual that teaches how to do Pluto, how to do Leo, etc. – she can read every single one of them. None of them will make total sense to her and she'll always be dissatisfied or feel that something's missing. If you say to somebody, "My Pluto's in Leo in the 5th," and that person says, "You a singer, dancer, painter?" They'll go through these typical Leo things that we think of as self-expression. "Are you a performer?" And you do some of those things, but the ways that other people have seen it in others, she just can't do it and feel authentic. So for example somebody says, "Oh really, you paint? What do you paint?" And if you say, "Acrylics." What do you paint with?

Candace: Everything.

Tom: Okay, so you say "acrylics" and that person has an idea of what that's about or watercolors is a better example here because there's a kind of aesthetic that seems to come with watercolors. You know, it's soft, it's pretty, and it's cute, and it's sailboats and bunnies or whatever. But that aesthetic is not dramatic. You might be painting your version of Bosch's painting of the demons in hell in like pink, blue, and yellow watercolors. Because your self-expression works a little differently. That person sees your painting and goes, "Oh my God, this is terrifying!" [audience laughs] You're just doing it differently because that's how you do it. But if you tried to paint the butterflies and the dandelions of a watercolor aesthetic that you might have seen represented somewhere, you'll end up thinking, "Well, that's stupid." You might even try to make it interesting and you can't do it. You added a bug – doesn't matter. Because it's not yours, your expression. You're modeling it after something else. So she's got to reinvent the wheel whatever the creative thing is. And because Saturn's there it also has to do with business. You might even look around to see how other people put on weekend intensives like this. You can gather data and it still won't be satisfying. You need to come up with your own way of doing it. That's the idea.

It also has to do with having, fostering, and sharing opinions – even on that basic level. Forget creativity – opinions. Someone asks, "Well, what do you think, Candace?" This Pluto-Saturn stuff comes out there. With the retrogrades, however she gives her opinion is going to be a little different because she has to figure out her own way. I might ask you your opinion and you might give me something that is genuine and authentic but I think is vague. You tell me it isn't and that I'm just hearing it that way because you expected something else. Do you know what I'm talking about?

Candace: Yes.

Tom: I want your personal input but since it's retrograde you're going to give me personal input that's a little different.

This is why everyone needs to learn astrology, so we can sit down with our families and our friends and our business partners and explain each other to each other.

Pluto is square Chiron in the 7th in Scorpio, which is retrograde, so there's an issue about the soul's mission of self-expression giving and getting friction from – being squared – by sensitive others, other people's feelings – Chiron in the 7th. On the personality level you carry Chiron in the 7th with the wound that goes with that, but this underlying soul's mission has you receiving friction from wounded others or other people's sensitivity. For example she might want to say, "I am now going to be bold – everybody, listen up." But she will be aware of the 3 people out of the 12 in the room who are hypersensitive to what she might be about to say. That's friction, squaring your mission. The soul's intention is to learn the right way to be bold in your own way and yet keep it in check because of your awareness of others.

I tend not to look much when looking at a chart in this way at sextiles and trines because people don't come in complaining about life issues that correlate to Pluto sextile Neptune or Pluto trine Ascendant. So I don't tend to focus on them because I'm looking for the juice, I want to know what's wrong and I want to help you fix it. But I am going to talk about this yod here involving Pluto quincunx retrograde Mercury and Mars in Pisces in the 12th. The soul's mission includes receiving a very uncomfortable, discomfiting aspect from these two planets in the 12th house.

One of the things to say about the 12th house and Pisces are that they have to do with the big picture. We can talk about the 12th house here on the personality level and talk about how Sun-Ceres and Mercury-Mars in the 12th comes out in the personality but when we talk about those two symbols – Mars and Mercury – quincunxing Pluto, there is something extremely uncomfortable that has gone down about her self-expression from information from the big picture. There's some kind of big reality check that makes her feel like she got pushed off track. A square leaves the feeling that you're pushed from the side, perhaps pushed over. You know, sometimes you get knocked off a horse you're riding – that's a square. With the quincunx, you get knocked off the horse, you twisted your ankle, you rolled down this little hill, hit your head on a rock, and the horse left. It knocked you off course, blindsided you, like you can't really get back on track, and it's harder to get back up. For you, Candace, this soul's mission of self-expression has been blindsided by something in the 12th house outside of your control that's big.

I don't know if I've told you this before but what I'm feeling now is – and I'm not reading you specifically but this is the energy we're talking about – say that you're an 11-year old girl. All you want to do is to be a dancer. You live in a time and place where people can become dancers. And then there's some giant flood that ruins everything. 30% of the people in your community die and you can't stay where you are. Your community has to run. But it's another 15 years before the community is re-established enough that people can feel free to focus on creativity and there's room for people to become dancers again, for the community to support and feed dancers – not just doing a jig after a long day's work. So your creative expression – your ability to express who you really are, perform yourself – is knocked off track by this Mars-Mercury, this water event from the 12th that knocks everything off course. Natural disaster is one possibility. In some other life it can be a person or a group but I'm feeling that energy of "It's outside my control." And it's 12th-house big. By the time you can get back up on the horse you have 6 kids and you're not going to be a dancer – it's over by the time you're 26 and the community is re-established somewhere else. The big thing here is that something big and out of her control knocked her off course. Can I ask you a question? Were you and your husband nomadic for a bit? For how long?

Candace: From the minute we were together until I got pregnant.

Tom: How many years?

Candace: 8 years.

Tom: That's a karmic echo of being on the go. In this life it was by choice, right? You preferred that?

Candace: We didn't know any different. Like if that's the way the wind blew, it's where we went.

Tom: There you go – *that's the way the weather took us, the wind took us.* So in some life it's necessity and feeling forced, and there's a karmic wound about your own self-expression because of the external thing you can't control.

Candace: Having to just go with it because that's where it went.

143

Tom: Exactly. For you at this stage in life, to have this kind of space to do your astrology thing – which is your 12th-house expression – as well as this space to be your studio, that is bringing to completion a couple of things from not having freedom. Can I ask you other questions? This might seem random but when you were younger did you have an age you didn't think you'd live past?

Candace: I wonder.

Tom: Did you ever imagine being the age you are now?

Candace: No.

Tom: That's what I'm getting at. But I'm thinking about it less literally about this particular age than your ability to look ahead, to have faith and hope in your own future. Because if your self-expression is at any point [draws finger in line over throat] then it can rob your will to live.

Candace: My friends have heard me say that.

Tom: I remember when I was in my 20s and I had a girlfriend who was a couple of years younger than me. She had a couple of crow's feet, tiny ones. She turned to me one day and said, "I am so happy about the prospect of gaining age and growing older." That made her happy and it threw me, and here with you I'm getting that image in my head when thinking about being on the run. And if you don't have freedom to express yourself with Pluto in the 5th, why even bother being here?

Back to the yod. Pluto is sextile Neptune. A yod is two bodies sextile each other and they are each 150 degrees from some planet or point. It's called a yod which is the

144

name of a Hebrew letter but it's also called a finger of God. Some people think of it as related to destiny though I would offer you that it's the *feeling* of destiny. Some would say that it feels like the finger of God is pointing at you to do something related to the symbol. So here we have a different level than the karmic analysis because we're talking about a focus on Mercury-Mars. Basically, we could say that Pluto and Neptune here get along (sextile) and they're pointing a very uncomfortable finger at Mercury-Mars. Candace is going to feel that Mercury-Mars in Pisces in the 12th is something she absolutely has to do but because of this karmic conditioning – the quincunx to Pluto – it might be hard to actually do it.

Candace: I don't even know what they're like.

Tom: A lot of pressure gets put on Mercury-Mars but because she's been burned by people and situations manifesting that energy it might be hard to do.

The South Node is in Sagittarius in the 8th house and in a wide conjunction to retrograde Jupiter in Scorpio also in the 8th. Again, and 8th-house South Node. Coming from environments where things get entangled, where maybe there's some codependency, maybe there's some intensity and drama, maybe there's a focus on sex, death, or other people's money. It's in Sagittarius so things that are happening there are happening in a Sagittarius way. There might be a lot of belief, or religion/philosophy or the lack of it, but it's shaped by belief and much about what relationships are about. That it's conjunct Jupiter says that the South Node environment is saturated with this energy but it's retrograde. And that Mars-Mercury in Pisces/12th is square the nodes as is Lucifer in Leo/6th. It's another story of being entangled with others and needing to learn how to detangle untangle things.

Jupiter on the South Node means that Candace is a pro at Jupiter and that it's on a Sagittarius South Node makes a heavier emphasis on Jupiterian themes. She already knows about it. The people she comes from do Jupiter well though it's retrograde and in Scorpio, the sign about seeing the truth. Did you tell me there was no religion in your family?

Candace: Not really.

Tom: Because they saw through it? Because it wasn't something that was appealing?

Candace: Right.

Tom: Did they read a lot of books? Or what did they do?

Candace: Bridge, golf.

Tom: Okay, enjoyment.

Summer: Our parents danced.

Tom: Okay, thanks.

Candace: Something was definitely behind the scenes.

Tom: A little secret something?

Candace: Yeah. Lots.

Tom: Let's look at the squares to the nodes. Mars is will, Mercury is communication and perception. These square the nodes represents an unresolved issue about the use of will and communication, but in the 12th house in Pisces, is the will aligned with something greater? I want to point out that with this the thought pattern of "I didn't know anything else; I just went where the wind took me" – is your will in that situation aligned with something greater or do you just stop having will? See the difference? For you it's good to learn the difference and to make choices that are aligned with something versus just surrendering to the wind. Pisces represents the mode of surrender and surrender is great – you have an emphasis there and you've got to do it. But karmically it's good for you to sort out what is the right use of will. Is this intention and action aimed in the right direction? With the quincunx to Pluto, a flood overpowers and you just go limp and let it do what it will and then you can lose self-assertion over time because you're always being overpowered and you're not sure how to do something or make choices. Do you see that? It's being swept away and becomes learned helplessness – the weather events are too big. Or the political movements or the whatever.

Annette: Is that like learned helplessness?

Tom: It can be, yeah. If you're always feeling overpowered by something much bigger than you you can realize that the path of least resistance is best, which here is going limp and surrendering anything you want. Just letting the world act on you.

Glenna: It doesn't feel good.

Tom: No, it doesn't. But it's a survival strategy that gets adopted later – that's the point. You do it and then the karma – the belief attached to it – can or could be that it's better not to struggle. You can tell me if that's a hit or miss. "These things are always overpowering – I can't struggle against this. I can't win." Then you end up feeling disempowered, right? 3rd chakra-2nd chakra disempowerment. So every time you make a choice, it helps heal that. Not a decision like, "Should I get out of the way now or in 5 seconds?" but "What do I really want?" Answering that makes a change.

For the karma that goes with that – the belief – what is the best thing to do? It is to examine the assumptions while recognizing that they are the results of experience in the past. Acknowledging it and being fair to you as a being who has been shaped by experience: you've learned. Great! You've evolved. But you've evolved in certain directions based on certain beliefs that don't end up serving you as a being. As a human in certain contexts that's what's needed to survive but not always.

Sometimes it will seem to part of you that you don't know what you want. Sometimes it's true but what could be happening sometimes is that there's a belief in play that it's better not to want because that tidal wave is on its way, from one source or another. Why bother wanting?

Candace: Something's going to come along and …

Tom: Destroy it. And that's 12th-house pain. Overpowered. It's almost like having Pluto there for you.

Candace: Yeah.

Tom: A deep wounding about the 12th house.

Jillian: I was looking at Mars in Pisces square the nodes so she's got to learn about that issue. But with this configuration conjunct retrograde Mercury and then in the yod with retrograde Saturn, retrograde Pluto, and retrograde Neptune so she has to learn to do those things her own individual way. Since Mars is not retrograde, is there some way that she can look to how people in her life exercise Mars and learn from them? Do you know what I'm saying?

Tom: Yes, and because it's with the Mercury that's retro the reasons for some of their actions might not work for you but the behaviors might.

Jillian: It's the one thing in the configuration that's not retrograde so maybe she can mirror others to learn how to do it.

Tom: So when I mentioned setting up a workshop like this, I said that you can do all the research but the retrograde thing requires that you make your own decisions. But some things that have happened and that people have done with workshops might work for you but your reasons for making the same choices would be different. If you ask others why they set theirs up that way, the reasons won't make sense to you but you can do some of the same things.

Jillian: You can use the same strategy.

Tom: Yes, but it might serve different purposes or motivations. It's kind of a minor point but if you want strategies to work with the Mars then it's not minor.

Candace: Yeah, to get strategies to work with my own will I can go to the places where I go, "Hey, that works – I like how you did that."

Tom: You might not appreciate their motivation.

Candace: I don't care about their motivation. It'll work for me. It feels good.

Tom: Perfect! The bottom line with this comment is that because the Mars is not retro –

Candace: I can do it my own way.

Tom: Yes, you can bring, transfer, apply, and translate.

Candace: I like this. This is huge.

Tom: So the karma here is a set of beliefs about why to do things and why not to do things. The emotional archaeology process on it is to feel what you just felt, what you allowed to come to the surface and are feeling it while you're processing what I'm saying – the emotional archaeology is in changing why the things happened. I said to you maybe a tidal wave or flood or whatever, but we might not know specifically what has happened, but something has overpowered you. Rewriting it in your head should involve instances from this life when you remember being overpowered and making that the object of the process, the focus. We don't know what happened.

Candace: I just know it's a feeling. A sensation, an assumption.

Tom: A feeling, right. So why did it happen? Because shit happens – weather events happen. That's why it happened, if it was a weather event. Why did it happen? It happened because you live on Earth – that's what happens here sometimes. There's no reason it happened related to anyone doing anything wrong. If the story about the girl who didn't get grow up to devote her life to art, creativity, and expression resonates with you, know that it didn't

150

mean that she wasn't worth experiencing that. But you can imagine the practicalities growing up in a family struggling to make ends meet with a kid who just wants to go daydream. They can't let the kid do it. "Go milk the whatevers, go do the chores" – got to do it. But then the kid can feel that they don't honor her creativity and they don't care about who she really is. Well, actually, they're just focused on survival, what they think is important then is survival. So that's the belief to change as far as the creativity goes. Necessity happens. Weather happens. Food has to get on the table. But it doesn't mean that your creative shininess is not important. It just means that something else had to happen for a while. So if you can rewrite that then you can change that karma.

The South Node ruler is Jupiter, which is on the South Node. It's in a different sign, Scorpio. So it's retro in Scorpio in the 8th. You come from people who are entangled and you're somebody who's liable to become entangled. You come from people who are focused on belief of some kind or at least goals or vision of something, or pleasure in this case when were talking about their hobbies and things they enjoyed pursuing – golf, dancing, and bridge being the 3 key words that came up –

Candace: And secrets.

Tom: But see, karmically you are in Scorpio – you're a detective. If they are trying to be Sagittarius, which is about going and doing something fun, you're sensing the stink in the closet. That's the friction in how you're a little different than they are.

Jillian: Can I go back to something you mentioned? You were talking earlier about the South Node ruler's relationship with the South Node. If the South Node ruler is conjunct the South Node then you fit with your family. But it's out of sign.

Tom: Yes, it's out of sign.

Jillian: So a different story. But on the surface did it appear that you were tight with them?

Candace: Yeah. It seemed like we were the crew for the queen and king. We were their little dancers.

Tom: The court.

Jillian: Everything seemed hunky-dory to other people?

Candace: Oh, yes. But it wasn't.

Tom: Sure, but that's not the point. Did you *feel* that you were tight together.

Candace: I think I felt it was a necessity. The tightness was based on some sort of secret, some sort of code or some sort of system.

Tom: That makes sense.

Candace: You couldn't break out of it.

Tom: Yeah, I see that.

Candace: I'm not really sure what it was all about.

Tom: You'll figure it out in this life.

Then I want to talk about the North Node a bit. The North Node in Gemini in the 2nd – again, a 2nd-house North Node. The need to pick through what's entangled and leave behind what doesn't work. To develop your own self-esteem. Your own reasons to feel good about you or do

152

anything. Also in Gemini, it has to do with opening up, becoming flexible, asking questions, and looking for things.

Candace: Curiosity.

Tom: Yes. I think one of the things I've said to you about this is that the Sagittarius South Node can get fixed on a belief about what's happening. The Gemini North Node says, "You're probably wrong – you need more data, more information, and less belief about what it is and more hearing the numbers, hearing the words, doing the research, turning the pages."

Candace: Being curious, learning, exploring.

Tom: Right, because everything you think is happening is just what you think is happening.

Glenna: You need to be amazed.

Tom: Yeah, exactly. Instead of "I've seen it all."

Candace: Being willing to experience wonder about it. Not being the skeptic.

Tom: Good. Obviously I'm not dealing with every aspect to these karmic indicators. I want to keep painting a picture for you of process and what it does. Does anyone have questions about using the method of analysis or about these two charts in particular?

Anne: I don't know how related it is, but is it your belief that as we do our own healing work that we're also healing our family of origin?

Tom: I do believe that. I think that each person will have a different focus of what that needs or looks like or means. But I do think so because we do carry family karma: "I've agreed to come here and perpetuate your genetic line

153

and you've agreed to welcome me." So we carry these threads of karma together. And because the South Node represents the families we pick, yeah. When we choose new things in relation to the family or shared karma there are two effects. One is behind the scenes of what we're carrying – we can transmute it. The other one is that we actually learn new things and can teach our family indirectly or directly. For Candace as an example, there's a Sagittarius thing running through her family system but if she does the Gemini thing, people are going wonder and be surprised – they'll notice it's different. They're going to ask her where she learned that and she'll reply that she got interested in something and asked her friend for advice/book from the library/book bought online. And the family might respond that they didn't know it was a topic. And then things can spread. How long have you been into astrology, Candace?

Candace: A long time.

Tom: How long has Summer been into astrology?

Summer: I'm just learning.

Tom: And how did you get interested?

Summer: Through Candace.

Tom: Gemini North Node – new data, new information. We know your charts are different, Summer, we know that you don't have a Sagittarius South Node. But there's a family link in that Summer learns something from Candace. New information, openings, data. Summer, you hear Candace speaking a new language and see the effect and think it might be worth exploring. You're personally

154

inclined to do it but you're also a member of a family system. And then that ripples out because how you think of yourself affects how you deal with your kids now.

I want to mention one other thing before we finish here. It's a thing that happens on the subtle energetic levels that we don't see or talk about. We're all picking up on a different corner of this big thing that the family has agreed to process. The lighter your load gets it does spread subtly through the system. Even after people die and evolve spiritually after death they can learn about the family system though how the individuals who are still alive are processing things. The dead see the big picture but I'm interpreting things through a lens I was trained to use and so they learn from my conscious awareness and how that changes, too. It's really spectacular. What a trip, what a game.

Tom: Something I hope you're all getting in here is how this jargon and the symbols relate to life even if you're not memorizing the jargon or feel schooled in it, you're seeing all this. For example, Michael, you know Candace well.

Michael: Yes, and you described something for her that I feel I've personally gone through, something that she's going through. So it was so relevant I almost could have thought you were talking to me. It helped me be informed about what something looks like versus what it is.

Tom: Good. There are also times when someone will hear something but in 10 or 15 years might go through it and there'll be a little remembrance. Maybe you'll hear the recording again later and make connections. Or something you're hearing about today you experienced years ago. That's why this format is so great – we're just talking about human stories even as we discuss someone's specific life. But this is real human stuff and you relate to what we talked about with Candace.

Glenna

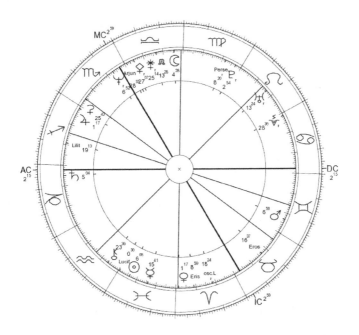

February 25, 1959, 3:54 AM, Seattle, WA

Tom: Let's start with Pluto as the soul's empowerment journey. There's a new archetype here we haven't talked about yet today; Pluto's conjunct the asteroid Persephone.[14] As a side note, I don't expect anyone else to use all these archetypes I use, like Persephone, Lucifer, and Arjunsuri. They answer questions for me. They bring in key word lists and stories that we live as they answer questions.

---

[14] Asteroid 399. See *Living Myth: Exploring Archetypal Journeys* for the full story.

Occasionally I get drawn to add something and I've been asked when I might stop, and I don't see it happening because, as we're going to see right now, they answer questions. Everything Glenna's heard about Pluto retrograde in Virgo in the 8th house will change with Persephone added to it. Just like Annette's Pluto conjunct Juno adds flavor – it's not just seeking expression, it's *committed* to the search. She didn't just check out two religions. She did a bunch for 3 years each.

It's our first Pluto in Virgo for the day and in the 8th house. The arena of life is trust, intimacy, where we join together, and then of course the pitfalls involve lack of trust, lack of intimacy, and codependent entanglement. That's the arena of life – where the soul is seeking to become empowered as Glenna. We know right off the bat that Glenna in all these different lives has all kinds of empowering experiences in various ways of approaching intimacy including in friendship and business dealings. Intimacy in the 8th house includes by the way the fact that your lawyer or accountant knows all the crap about your finances, in addition to friends who know your secrets and lovers who know all kinds of intimate things about you. In different lives she has a lot of empowering experiences about truth, openness, honesty, and trust but she's also got a lot of disempowering experiences. Before we look at the chart we don't know where she lands on this spectrum of empowered to disempowered. We just know that over the course of thousands of lives she's been all over the range. We don't know exactly where she landed this week or last month but we know she has a lot of experience in this. The Pluto is retrograde, so she's got to invent her own wheel for this and do her own thing.

In Virgo, the core mission is analysis, improvement, service, and developing a relationship with duty and responsibility. It's about 1958 to 1971 and it's not that all of them are responsible but at the soul level they're seeking to become empowered through exploring responsibility. The biggest slobs and the biggest neat freaks are in that generation. The most humble servants and also the most arrogant people who refuse to serve are in that generation because they're exploring this Virgo stuff from all sides. That's the basic idea.

Adding Persephone to it. Wherever Persephone is in the chart we need to be abducted into new ways of being.

Michael: Abducted into.

Tom: Abducted.

Michael: Taken away. Stolen away.

Tom: [whispering] Stolen away. Taken.

Michael: Kidnapped.

Tom: Kidnapped. Literally or figuratively, by self or other – but yes. Yeah, it's very juicy. When it shows up with Pluto, it's very juicy. [group laughs]

In the myth, Persephone (or Proserpine) is the daughter of Ceres (or Demeter), who is the harvest goddess, and is the prototypical daughter or maiden: innocent, teenager kind of energy. And protected by the mother to the point of overprotection. Her father is Zeus (or Jupiter). He's kind of all over the place, kind of loose morals, his ethics are kind of questionable. He isn't really looking out for her but her uncle, who is Hades (or Pluto), the lord of the underworld, sees her and falls in love. Hades goes to his brother the father of Persephone and says, "I want to marry your daughter." Zeus/Jupiter says, "Mom will *never* go for this. We're gonna have to figure out a trick." Zeus goes to Gaia, the Earth goddess, and has her create a new flower because being a maiden, Persephone has spent a lot of time with all the beautiful flowers. She knows all the flowers, so creating a new flower is to get her spend time in one place so that Pluto can come and kidnap her.

She's lingering at this wonderful flower that no one has ever seen before – she's marveling, she's smelling. A crack in the Earth opens up and Pluto comes up, snatches her away, and takes her to the underworld to be his bride. In this story, literal abduction.

It seems like she's his prisoner but I think she's just there. Not that she knows how to get out but we don't have any indication that he is holding her captive in the way we might expect. He wants her to want to marry him. Eventually she eats 1 or 6 pomegranate seeds, depending on the source, and that is essentially making a deal to stay – she in effect marries him by eating these pomegranate seeds. They're tiny and we might think them insignificant but since she eats something, a transaction takes place. She through this becomes the queen of the underworld, the queen of the dead, and is ushered into maturity. That's the big thing.

Mom freaks out on the surface and appeals to the gods. There's this big hullabaloo wherein she claims this is unfair and unjust, but let's see Persephone's perspective, too. Persephone just got launched very suddenly into maturity. In the culture we live in we might be afraid of actual abduction of children and it is something that happens, and to adults as well. But the main point with this Persephone story as we live it is that we need to be ushered into new realities; we need to snatched out of comfort zones and into maturity.

This asteroid is also retrograde with the retrograde Pluto. Glenna in different lives is going to have experiences being abducted into very intimate 8th house relationships. It can be the sudden presence of someone who is like the lord of the underworld and she says, "Wow! I'm ready for that." Or it can be not feeling ready but feeling that she has to do it, or it can be a seduction – literal or figurative, romantic or not, but snatched out of safe contexts. It's retrograde, so when she looks at the idea of abducting the self she will not be able to find anyone else's model of it that works for her. Her abduction of self might look very different than everybody else's.

Are we all seeing this Persephone story? Good. Basically, we look at the person who was abducted in the myth and we feel terribly for her. We feel that she was snatched away, raped, and held captive. But the reality is that she was snatched away by somebody who loved her and wanted to exalt her, and the only way he knew how was to make her his queen. But we fear the underworld:

anything but the underworld. We look at him as a dark figure but as we've been talking about today, absolute self-knowledge, owning your motivations, and self-acceptance leads to Plutonian empowerment. If we do this then Pluto doesn't have to be that bad and we can come to no longer fear for Persephone. We can choose not to fear the loss of innocence because it means the gaining of adulthood. And you can be an adult in all the ways that fit with this story – even sexuality and marriage – but you can be abducted into a truthful friendship. Glenna can be abducted into a gazing connection with a friend. And it can be sudden and dramatic, like the crack opening in the Earth. It can also be finding herself in a certain context and realizing she can't live in that way anymore (whatever it is) and she has to abduct herself into a new way of life.

So that's wrapped up in the soul's intentions. They have to do with learning through this inequality – Persephone being abducted involves inequality – and then learning how to abduct yourself into things that work well. That's a big part of the soul's mission. But it's in Virgo so there's an element of needing to analyze and choose; make active choices so you don't feel victimized. That is going to be at least some of the cache of what you find when you do emotional archaeology and dig down about beliefs about intimacy, relationships, truth, and trust. There are going to be some knots with labels on them that have to do with somebody causing you to be launched into a new reality. When the truth is that you are a powerful, Divine creator – you are already Goddess and God – and all abductions

162

serve your journey. The soul has said, "I need to be abducted until I learn how to abduct myself into better realities."

Glenna: I forgot that but remember now.

Tom: Did we talk about it in your sessions? I don't know if I was using Persephone when we talked.

Glenna: No, but I have layers of meaning to go with it now since we talked the last time.

Tom: Understood. I think I would have remembered this if I'd been using Persephone then. You know, these asteroids sometimes come in and out of my practice and Persephone's in there for good but there was a time when she wasn't.

That's a basic level of this Pluto. But looking at the process of Pluto in Virgo over many lives, this element of becoming empowered through making choices is important. It's about classifying and categorizing, and analyzing, and then making a choice about where your energy's going to go. We can know that in many lives and in a portion of this life you have not made choices about where your energy goes, so the abductions have seemed random and chaotic, leaving you wondering why you would ever choose what you experienced.

We do have some other aspects that are important here. Two squares, a quincunx, and two oppositions. I might not spend as much time on each of these as we did for that last one but I do want to give you a couple of sentences on each one.

Pluto square Mars: learning about Mars by receiving friction from Mars. Look at the energy of Pluto in Virgo in the 8th squared by Mars in Gemini in the 5th. In Virgo/8th you're pretty serious about getting the truth out and Gemini/5th is pretty serious about not sitting still and not being open – perhaps scattered. So you'll draw people to you over many lives who don't focus, who are like a bird fluttering around, and that can make you feel you can't achieve the mission of the seriousness. Because Virgo/8th needs time and Gemini/5th will not give it to you.

Jillian: Could you elaborate on that?

Tom: Yeah. The 8th house done in a Virgo way requires analyzing what creates intimacy. But Gemini in the 5th house is going to be flexible about everything and wanting to have fun. The 5th house is not about sitting down and looking each other in the eye for prolonged periods. There's a natural square between these two houses is what I'm getting at, and also the two signs.

Jillian: Is Mars in Gemini in the 5th other people, or her?

Tom: It's going to be other people manifesting the lesson for her.

Jillian: Because it's square?

Tom: Because we all have other people manifesting each of the symbols. She will draw people to her for the illustration but if she gets it then she doesn't have to do that anymore.

Jillian: With the seriousness, and this square as tension – the seriousness is *not* Mars in Gemini in the 5th.

Tom: That's what I'm getting at. But with Pluto, the seriousness, the stakes are high and the roots run so deep that Mars people doing that Gemini thing to her is karmic friction. And this is kind of the end of the story but for her to own the soul's intention – to learn about Mars by not being able to pin Mars down, which is a way of saying you have to stay flexible and be able to take in new information. Mars people are going to bring you new things and you'll think or ask, "Can we sit here and talk about this for 3 hours?" and Mars is going to say, "no."

On a different level, Mars squaring Pluto: assertion and aggression squaring your mission. I'm not trying to pry into your history but there are people who have this who have experienced overt abuse. Can I ask that? You have?

Glenna: Yeah.

Tom: Is that when growing up in your family, or is that later in relationship?

Glenna: I was sexually abused when I was really little, right off the bat. And then I picked husbands … one of the husbands stole money, another one abused the children.

Tom: Pluto-Persephone in the 8th square Mars in the 5th. When you're a child and then when you have children – it's an echo, if it suits their souls' journeys as well and also the people who did the things – it's a holographic representation in your life of Mars square Pluto. When I say that your soul is learning about Mars being squared by it, it's sufficient to say that for learning about this aspect but I want to say something else for you – it's not enough. We come back to the meaning assigned to why things happen. Frankly, people hurt each other all the time. Bu the meaning is what perpetuates it in other lives. So there's a life for you where – can we do this?

Glenna: Yes.

Tom: There's a life where you crave the deep connection that is indicated by this Pluto in the 8th, and you are prepared to open on every level. That's what you're ready for. Then there is the reality of how the people who are available to you are trained to interact with others. I'm just going to say this: this is kind of a careless, quick fuck when you have been opening your heart toward somebody for months. The soul learns through that, and frankly has learned all it can possibly learn through that. The reality of the events in your life and the lives of your kids obviously are important in looking at why the souls would draw that experience. It also has to do with the contracts between people at the soul level, including the contracts you have with your kids. What you learned because of and after the experiences that you had as a child – you and your kids share karma, which is why it happened to each of you. The birth order has a lot to do with this. So you experienced this when very young.

One of the ways that you are a teacher for them is because you also had this experience but you had it in a different time-space context and it was a different relationship. You see all this? You've already seen all this?

Glenna: Mm-hm.

Annette: Someone with that placement might really have a problem with trusting the self when it comes to intimate relationships?

Tom: That could be one way it manifests, thank you. I'd like to hear the process you went through to get to the place where you trusted yourself again. I can tell you're there now. Is there anything to share about that?

Glenna: It's just been about trusting myself to know that the soul's journey is more important than pleasing other people. There was a part of me before that thought that in order to be complete I had to have a partner. I think that's a big piece, as well as we went through as a family a huge healing around me apologizing for my blindness to my kids' experiences of abuse as a result of my own. I hadn't owned up to theirs. I had picked it in order to echo in order for us to heal that, in my view. I mean, I was numb to it but then we apologized and I said, "I'm sorry. I didn't mean to be blind to what you were going through but I couldn't be present to it because of my own." And then I chose to go ahead and enter my own process of healing and then I could be present to theirs.

Tom: That is *the* karmic journey with this Pluto. When we do experience something terrible, if we shut down we can't even see the reality around us. Part of your Pluto in Virgo is learning responsibility. Unconsciously and unwittingly putting yourself in situations where you cannot be as responsible as you would want to be – you just can't do it.

The other square to Pluto is from Ceres in Scorpio and Jupiter in Sagittarius. A square to Ceres here will have an element of not being safe. As far as it being in the 11th, it's kind of somebody's idea of where things should be headed, where things should go brings friction to your need to connect. It will manifest in a bunch of different ways. For example some Jupiterian person that you draw to you focusing on where his or her life is headed giving friction to your need to be real and connect.

The oppositions are to Sun-Lucifer. With Pluto opposing Sun whatever this mission is about is blocked by people who shine pretty brightly and cannot be moved. With the soul's intention being to learn about what true strength and power are but the long, slogging process is of fighting power and trying to figure out how powerful you really are. If you're in Virgo and being opposed by someone in Pisces, they're slippery. You can't put your finger on what they're about or wrap your mind around the effect they have on you. The opposition to something in Pisces has you looking someone right in the eye and it can feel like, "I'm looking right at you but I can't figure out your name, where you come from, what you want" – this elusive, slippery thing. But here it's the Sun so it's big and in the 2nd house, it's not movable. More grounded than you perceive you might be or could turn out to be. It's a power struggle but the truth is the Pluto is the real marker of power, but we've been learning through duality so we're working with a faulty conception of strength. To be powerful – to feel strong and confident – if you need truth and honesty and but you're opposed by somebody who won't work with you, you might feel robbed of your power. You said earlier that you had felt you needed a partner. What you need is truth and honesty. Partners come and go. Or you can say "yes please" or "no thanks." But what you need is honesty and to have that commitment to yourself to stay present even though that pain exists.

Group: Could you rephrase that?

Tom: In order for Glenna to feel strength relative to this Plutonian soul's mission, she cannot not have truth. It requires honesty within relationship to feel strong – according to one way of doing it, until she changes her mind and knows that she can be that way by herself. It's kind of like the blind spot, the default need, the assumption that comes from Pluto in the 8th. And the 8th house is where we come together in the most intense, intimate ways. Lots of people with Pluto in the 8th don't spend a lot of time alone, out of relationship, or they spend their whole lives outside relationship so they don't have to be up against others in intense, intimate ways – joined at the hip, conjoined, intertwined, and entangled because it's too painful. *Why go there? It's too painful – can't deal.* For the first bit of my practice I had people with Pluto in the 8th come in for readings and they wouldn't tell me what they wanted to work on. It was an interesting pattern and then it broke, but they would ask me to tell them what I see. "Well, I see you have trust issues." Anyway.

And then Pluto is quincunx Venus. Remember the idea of the quincunx indicating one being pushed off course. As I said to Candace it's not just that you fell of the horse but all these dumb little tragedies compounded and left you feeling like helpless for a time, knocked off course, derailed. This is happening with Venus in Aries. I see sudden information from somebody who was important to you – Aries in the 3rd. Something that just broke a dam, that surprised. This is an energy her soul needs to learn about as her soul intends to learn about Venus – which is fairness, harmony, equality, balance but also value system and what's really important to a person – intending to learn about those things through getting knocked off course by them. The evolutionary intention with a quincunx to Pluto I would offer is to keep us on our toes: there is always a new piece of information that we never expect and don't want, but that's how growth happens. The karma of what happened when the blow was delivered – *that's* the thing to work on because this aspect is just a way to keep you on your toes. With Venus in Aries/3rd there is something fresh, original, and new in relationships that can keep you from getting entrained in this deep gazing. One of the effects it can have is to make you realize how important it is for you to have that time and that deep connection but not make other people wrong if they can't do it with you. To see the contrast: *I keep drawing people who are not on the same page* – a quincunx can offer the feeling that they can't be in the same room together. But why? To keep you on your toes. Because there are people who quincunx you with whom you get along really well. You know what I mean? So you being clear about what's important to you with Pluto in the 8th versus what's coming to you.

Jillian: I'm wondering if given more time, if this were a whole reading, if you … I find it compelling that Jupiter is conjunct Ceres and then Persephone is conjunct Pluto – they're all linked here and in their stories. Because of the juice of the story, would you tend to go into that more?

Tom: In principle no but if I asked her what she wanted to work on and the answer was about one of the themes wrapped up in this story that's emphasized with all four bodies in aspect, I probably would.

Jillian: Would you talk about the mother and the father and their interests here?

Tom: I would talk about that if it fit the story presented by the client. I don't tell every story I could tell. What I do is study the chart – the energy and the karma – and then I wait for the person to tell me what he or she wants to work on. With this chart, if Glenna came in to me and said, "I really want to talk about my job," that's what we'd talk about even though I've looked at Mars square Pluto-Persephone, Jupiter-Ceres square Pluto, etc. Even though I'm looking at the underworld journey. I prep fully and look at all the themes and then honor what you want to work on.

Glenna: I feel compelled to share this. My dad died before I was born in a helicopter crash. He threw his energy to my mom because she was 2 months pregnant with me and he wasn't ready to go. My sense is that he was wrapped around my energy cord to stay close to my mom. It felt to me like an abduction in that my sense of him being there in the womb with me – on a soul level of course it was known this was going to happen – but it feels like, "Hey! What are you doing here?" I wasn't alone in the womb, you know?

And then the connection with my mom, about the Ceres-Jupiter. They wanted to be together energetically so they kind of did it through me. And then I had a very hard time recently when he left me – he's gone now. Two years ago. And I've never made that connection before with the themes of abduction. Gulp.

Tom: It's interesting. How rare to see those 4 bodies in that kind of relationship together. Mother and father and then the underworld couple.

Candace: Wouldn't that be about the karmic family wound, this situation with Pluto?

Tom: The South Node would focus more on the family. She has contracts with people at the soul level but the Pluto wound is really hers, what she brings in. That it squares Ceres indicates her wounding through family, so yes.

Candace: And the Moon on the North Node.

Tom: Yeah. Let's go to the nodes, the second step. The South Node is in Aries in the 3rd conjunct Lilith and Eris. We haven't talked about Eris yet. She is the goddess of strife and discord. She is not invited to this big-deal wedding on Mt. Olympus to which every other deity is invited and is hurt. She has this golden apple fashioned and on it is inscribed "for the fairest" and throws it in the middle of the reception knowing that three goddesses who have been invited would bicker over it.

Eris's insecurity about not getting invited to the party makes her take action to stir the insecurities of others but it's all because she's hurt. This whole thing leads to the Trojan War, that giant conflict. Zeus is appealed to to make the decision about which of the three goddesses is the fairest because they are bickering, according to the story as it comes to us. He won't do it – he's the consummate politician and knows that if he makes one friend here he makes two enemies. Instead Zeus brings in Paris, a mortal who Zeus says is very fair, wise, just, and has great powers of judgment. Paris is offered a bribe from each of the three goddesses and he picks the bribe best suited to him, the most beautiful woman in the world. That's Helen of Troy and she's already married, and you know the rest of the story. Then Helen is stolen away by Paris with Aphrodite's help and the Trojan War, the biggest armed conflict on Earth, is the result. It all starts with someone who didn't get invited to a party. [group laughs]

So, Eris is about pushing people's buttons, perhaps unintentionally, with strife, discord, and tension that's buried comes to the surface and not knowing what to do with it. Eris conjunct the South Node says that there is some chaos in the family system that has to do with Mars. Can I ask you a question about the abuse? Was this person in your family?

Glenna: No. Mine was a neighbor, theirs was the man that I married.

Tom: Their stepfather?

Glenna: Yes.

Tom: So there's some chaos, unprocessed pain, and insecurity that's floating around in the family system including not doing Aries-style protection. That's the theme: *we can't protect each other.*

Glenna: Right.

Tom: It feels to you like a betrayal but it's really an inability to look out for you. They're dealing with their emotional thing just as you as an adult were dealing with your emotional thing.

Glenna: I just felt like I betrayed my kids.

Tom: You didn't feel that you were betrayed?

Glenna: I haven't felt like that.

Tom: Okay.

So that's the thing with Eris – strife. Lilith is also on the South Node and I talked earlier about instinct, connection to lower chakras, and the wisdom of the Earth coming through the body. But here we are living in patriarchal reality and so Lilith lots of times – especially karmically – represents inequality in relationships, that the woman shouldn't open her mouth, or if she does she's probably going to get punished. It's kind of a stereotype but that's part of our patriarchal history and you're coming in to this life with that karma. In Aries, there's a lot going on. There's always something happening that has to be responded to. The 3rd house is the house of mind, learning, and perception but it's also the house of curiosity and exploration. With Aries in the 3rd things can always be happening rapid-fire – and never stop. The house of Mercury colored by Mars. That's the kind of karmic history background she's coming from. There's chaos – stuff has to be responded to. There's inequality. People feel underserved and unprotected, and probably unloved as a result.

There is one square to the nodes, which is Saturn in Capricorn in the 1st. We're talking about the family system as opposed to you. There is confusion about responsibility, maturity, morality, and ethics. There's a lack of leadership coming from this chaos with Aries in the 3rd house. The karmic imprint of Saturn square the nodes is about not being sure how to be the right kind of adult. Very often this comes with very clear ideas but they are not enough to make you feel successful, happy, or healthy. We had this in our very first conversation a couple of years ago with me as Saturn in which you confronted me: "I don't feel safe. This is not what I expect." And me saying, "You're creating a situation in which you don't feel safe. Let's talk about that instead because I'm not responsible for your experience." That was the first conversation we had, before she set up her reading. I was dealing with this part of you that feels unprotected, underserved, and not nurtured.

Glenna: It was a part that needed to stand up for my own needs. That was growing up for me that I communicated to you that I didn't feel … it wasn't meeting my need for … but I was so proud of our interaction. I was being brutally honest and you were responding and we worked through it. I felt so good about it but it was hard, too. It was messy.

Tom: It was. I was thinking, "Do you want a reading or not?" And then I realized what was happening: "She's going to have a reading but this is the just the beginning of it; this is just where it starts, a week ahead of time." So you're naturally going to have those questions because the people that you come from don't know how to do Saturn, Capricorn, or the 1st house responsibly. It's the family system – a lack of leadership. Therefore a lack of organization, a lack of direction, focus, a lack of creating a nurturing environment that makes people feel contained, right? It's also about recognizing potential and encouraging you – that kind of stuff, too.

Glenna: And the Saturn figure left. The father left.

Tom: Exactly. So she'll have karma – which are the beliefs – about what the right kind of adult should be like. Some of those beliefs will be inspired by what she didn't have but wishes she had. Some of them will be inspired by things she suspects could be good but hasn't tried out yet. Some of them will be tried and true from experience. But she'll have this variety. How she develops maturity and responds in a concrete way to reality is going to be determined by this set of beliefs and how much weight goes to different areas.

Again, I think of squares to the nodes as trial-and-error things because if we do this thing 5 times in a row and it doesn't work, the solution is not just to stop trying. I can imagine you when you're 14, starting to feel like you're starting to be an adult but can't do something because you don't know how and nobody can teach you to do it. You might feel something like, though not with this wording, "How can I possibly be empowered to do this thing for myself if nobody can teach me?"

Glenna: Kind of like you're on your own.

Tom: Yes. We're also talking about beliefs about what adults are like.

The last thing to talk about with the nodes is the Moon conjunct the North Node. A basic key word for Moon can be happiness, and that's as far away from your family system as possible. It's in Libra – communicating, harmony, getting on the same page, calming down. I know I've talked about that with you before with the apparent chaos related to this South Node and the Moon on the North Node and Saturn square the nodes. Part of you might think that there's no time to enjoy things. The music thing for you is a great thing for Moon on the North Node, by the way. It's other things, too, but it's a great way to slow down.

Moon conjunct North Node says that the people that her soul has chosen to train her, to be born to, aren't quite sure how to feel like they're in it together, either, because Moon is also how we connect with each other. It can be an assemblage of people who aren't sure why they're even related. It doesn't mean they don't feel inextricably tied together but maybe not getting the point. Like what were family dinners like in the house you grew up in?

177

Glenna: Yeah. I had a stepfather and then two half-brothers and I just remember I was longing for the same last name as my family. I'm accessing a lot of lifetimes when I was an orphan and had to be charming enough to be accepted. So a lot of this, "there isn't enough and I have to make it okay." And then things that are blind-siding, like, "I didn't know you expected that of me," and I'm kicked out. All the quincunxes tell me there are all kinds of things that are just coming at me that I didn't expect. The Libra on the North Node just keeps telling me that it's okay and I can calm down, go with the flow and allow that – to come out of the chaos, basically. But I like the chaos. I'm actually good at it. I love it.

Tom: Of course you are! But it turns into an option you have.

Glenna: Right, instead of thinking that I have to do it.

Tom: Or that you don't have a choice – that feeling of being trapped – which is being a little kid in a family where you don't have the same last name and that's all you want – trapped.

Glenna: Wanting to belong, and do what's right – the good girl, Saturn on the Ascendant.

Tom: You're talking about being charming in these other lives to be accepted. When you do that, it's a disingenuous Libra Moon.

Glenna: Yes, because then it's not congruent. I was voted most likable in the senior class. I probably wasn't being very real but I just needed to be liked.

Tom: It's good you have those insights from those other lives as an orphan.

Glenna: And then there was a life as a lone ranger where I got pushed off a cliff because I was trying to translate material rather than fighting, and nobody understood. A lot of being misunderstood, not fitting in. Working hard but it's not enough.

Tom: One of the things about Moon is that when it functions almost anywhere but on the North Node it can represent acceptance – always finding people who accept you no matter what even if you're not related to them. But the Moon on the North Node indicates a soul's intention to not have it.

Candace: Acceptance.

Tom: Yeah. How many people do you know who don't get along with their families but have friends who are like family? All of us? Many of us have that experience but when the Moon is on the North Node it's a karmic setup for needing to learn what it means to connect. And your soul is basically asking the people you're born to not to be able to accept you.

Glenna: And that's the catch.

Summer: So you can accept yourself.

Tom: And then learn to create family on her own and for the right reasons, for Libran reasons. *Because I want you to hear me and I want to hear you – I was us to be together and not because we happen to have genetics in common and we're sitting in the same house.*

Glenna: It does feel like the brick wall of reality in my life. My mom cannot understand – we totally miss each other. There's absolutely no connection there.

Tom: Can we focus on her for a minute as a space holder of this energy for you?

Glenna: Yes.

Tom: What does it mean that that's true?

Glenna: It's forced me to find my own acceptance of myself. The Moon in Libra has meant that I have had to give myself the acceptance that I need to find outside from my mother or whoever else I wanted to get it from. And learn to be my own battery pack and plug into my own higher self for the nurturing I needed.

Tom: And when you were younger what did it seem to mean? What did you believe it meant?

Glenna: It was really painful. That I was flawed, I was a misfit, I didn't deserve it somehow. There's something wrong with me. If I could only do enough or say the right thing. But I've realized that it will never be enough because it's not – well, we don't have the same values.

Tom: Let me offer you something or insert something into this. You get to the place where it's never enough, but there's a gap and it feels like something is falling short. I would love for you to be able to go to the next level with why it happens. The karma and soul contracts of adoption, fostering, and being an orphan is very specific – what a soul learns through that.[15] It's different for each case and

---

[15] See Understanding Loss and Death for an exploration of adoption and soul-level contracts and intentions.

180

part of the reason for adoption is that family groups might have a certain kind of relationship in one life. There can be two separate family groups who live on neighboring parcels of land or two tribal groups that are next to each other and they might as a group of souls have an agreement for certain kinds of transactions. In some life it can end up being that something terrible happens to one group and adoption can be for giving one family an opportunity to raise a child of the other group. This, by the way, could also be the section of that book about which the client became convinced that I had lost my mind because adoption was one of her experiences, too, and it can be very difficult to look at in this way. But for someone else to have the opportunity to offer you love even if they don't – but agreements between family systems. They can come about because of karma among the family, within the family system. One of the examples Djehuty uses in that section of that book is a family with 13 children and they can consistently feed 8 of them. So what do they do? If someone leaves – or 5 leave – the rest of them can rationalize but not really. They had to give up their loved ones. Later, in some other life circumstance happens and somebody can't have or keep a child. It looks like this American couple from Baltimore just flew to China to adopt this little girl who's 2½ years old. We say, "Oh, look at that!" and not seeing the karmic history that could have taken place on some other continent thousands of years ago that explains why this particular agreement, why this couple, why this family, why China, why here. It is always the opportunity to love each other but if you have Moon on the North Node you are seeking to learn what family is. This life you don't have the literal orphan thing but it is part of this history. There's a rich thing in there about learning what family is about. What we learn as adults what family is about – as we create family around us – is about absolute, utter self-acceptance, unconditional love, and total support and acceptance. But it could be easy for somebody in that situation to feel abandoned by life, God, or the people who can't keep you.

Glenna: It's a type of anger.

Tom: Yeah. Some people I know who have this experience in different lives have a heavy 12th house emphasis because they're learning the truth about how things really work here in this dimension. There's a particular thread or track of where love comes from, which you maybe wouldn't think of with the 12th house – like where love comes from – because we talk about power, powerlessness, surrender, mysticism, etc. But the truth of how things work here involves what is love. Well, you get to be the source of love but when you're a little kid and get taken away from a family you explore these questions in that way. I find it interesting.

So next is the South Node ruler Mars in Gemini/5th. We talked about it in terms of the square to Pluto and this is the second layer. It's aspected by half the chart and is the finger of a yod, so the finger that God is pointing at you to do something.

Glenna: The hugest part for me right now is developing the courage to be myself.

Tom: In what arena?

Glenna: Whatever it is that it means to be me. [group laughs]

Candace: Better be fun!

Tom: Yeah, it's got to be fun.

This yod – Saturn and Neptune grouping up over there pointing fingers at Glenna – the pressure! The incredible pressure to express the self but to loosen up enough to be able to do it. But it's about taking action to express the self. Candace has the Pluto-Saturn in Leo and will energetically, naturally draw opportunities, will draw people like me who say, "Please make a decision about what you want business-wise and then let me know." But for you, Glenna, half the chart is pressing on it. It's not like opportunities naturally come. You feel that if you don't do it, something's going to explode.

Glenna: Right.

Tom: It's enough to have a yod and then it's also the T-square business with Sun and Pluto. Oh, look – and the opposition to Jupiter. So your role within these different environments involves feeling singled out … for no reason. Now why would a soul do that?

Glenna: For the person to learn to honor their own truth and values, unless you have something else.

Tom: I like that. I might interview you instead of telling you. I might want to draw it out of you instead of telling you what I think. I want to see what else you're thinking.

All this pressure to *do* something. Why would a soul – oh, I just got the answer.

Glenna: I love your face!

Tom: I'm fishing, figuring if you get the answer you'll interject and if I get the answer I'll share what I got. But why would this soul do that? Coming from an Aries South Node where there's chaos, where you don't feel empowered to choose things because you're responding, you're putting out fires, everything's an emergency, somebody's always scraping a knee, breaking a vase.

Annette: It's conditioning.

Tom: Conditioned to chaos, yeah. And you get to the place where you don't choose. So this is a setup to find yourself in chaos and then realize that you can't do it but you have to do something, and then getting the impetus to go do it. That's interesting.

So square to Pluto is about learning about power by being squared by it. Pluto square Sun: learning about shining by being squared by it.

Jillian: Mars square Sun?

Tom: It's like being squared by something that's very shiny and big, and Sun's bigger than Mars, so it's the feeling of being squared by somebody powerful. In her various lives she's going to be caught in the middle – T-square – between Pluto and Sun energies arguing with each other. The kind of underworld power – big but maybe quieter – versus a louder, solar power, fire power, squaring each other and she's caught in the middle. If we looked at the tensions in her home growing up we would see that manifest in stepfather and mother or some other way, including with the half-siblings.

With the opposition to Jupiter in the 11th, you're learning about having a goal and balancing it with self-expression. The way you expand, are big, and reach out – Jupiter – is in the 11th house but that opposes this marker of her role which is in the house of individual creativity. With the South Node ruler opposed by Jupiter in the 11th there's this thing about needing to balance present and future. *You need to do this now but you also need to think about the future. But don't let your thought or belief about the future stop you from taking time out now to express yourself and play.* Jupiter in Sagittarius in the 11th coupled with the Saturn in Capricorn in the 1st square the nodes says that if there is any part of you inclined to be a workaholic, look at why. What is the goal? That in some other lives at least – I don't get the sense that it's this life overly much because I heard you sing last night and you're already open – but that karmic setup of perhaps not giving time to the self-expression because something has to get done. Like *something else needs to go – we need movement here. Who am I to be selfish and want to play my guitar?*

Glenna: Right.

Tom: But you've already processed that because you're doing it.

Glenna: Right.

Tom: Okay, good. [sound of helicopter overhead]

Glenna: That feels auspicious.

Audience: What was your father's name?

Glenna: Glenn.

It's the courage to speak truth integrating with the Jupiterian/11th house – connecting those two energies. At this point something about having the courage to use all of that and take it in a direction that it wants to go, but still in that sense of balance in the fun. It's kind of an echo – the Moon in Libra with that 5th house Mars in Gemini, so it's gotta be fun, you know? Work hard but it's fun. I feel Candace's Saturn in the 5th with work and the invitation to integrate it.

Tom: Well, what's courage?

Glenna: For me it's been facing something that I wasn't sure I could do every day, taking a baby step. Being courageous in taking one more step – like posting something on Facebook that all my Christian friends will think is of the devil. [group laughs]

Michael: It takes courage.

Glenna: Facebook's a good place to practice that.

Candace: Yeah, it is.

Tom: Because there's karma about courage in here, too, to dig into.

Glenna: There's something about being blind sided when I was courageous and stepped out. I mean I'm sure I've been on both sides of the fence but I feel it in my back and my kidneys right now, a burning as soon as you said that you were silenced, in a way that came from behind. So having courage has that feeling that I'm going to get killed and it will come from some place you didn't expect.

Jillian: Pluto in the 8th?

Glenna: Yeah.

Tom: In talking about emotional archaeology – you know, dusting this off and handling it gently and gingerly and looking at how to file it – why you get killed sometimes.

Glenna: In the bigger picture?

Tom: Why?

Glenna: Because I'm pissing people off?

Tom: That's the human-eyes perspective.

Glenna: Well, because my soul wants to push itself and go to the next lifetime?

Tom: That's what it looks like to all of us but that's not really it. One level is that you are giving the opportunity to certain other souls that your soul loves to overpower you to the point that your life is ended.

Glenna: Why would they want to do that?

Tom: Why would *they* want to do that?

Glenna: Why would I want to give them the power to do that?

Tom: Because your soul loves them.

Glenna: Am I a masochist?

Tom: Souls can only love each other. And every soul does not set out to complete its journey. Every soul sets out to support other souls in their journeys. It's one-sided because every soul – portions of the Divine Intelligence – has absolute, utter, unflinching, unwavering faith that everybody else is doing exactly what he or she needs to learn. So if you can make peace with those deaths you can change the karma of fearing somebody sneaking up on you from behind. It didn't happen because you said this or that.

Glenna: It was more of a contract with – like I was intentional about really wanting to provide that opportunity?

Tom: Yes, and in other lives someone else gives you the opportunity to overpower them – perhaps not through death. Perhaps through proselytizing a teaching. You have missionary karma, don't you?

Glenna: Yes.

Candace: How do you know that?

Tom: I can smell it.

Candace: No, Glenna – how do you know it?

Glenna: I just feel I was silenced. I was on a mission and I remember that that wasn't appropriate, people didn't want to hear it. And that feels missionary-like to me.

Tom: Yeah. So then the other thing – to dust *that* off – why would they not want to hear it? Does that mean the message is unimportant? So this is the process. We're just naming things right now but this is the process to do emotional archaeology. Anything that has an emotional charge will be accompanied by a belief, which is the label on the knot or the file folder. So just tell that inner detective that when this comes up and you're talking about the feeling and the burning in the kidneys – that's the red flag for me. I go right away to, "Let's talk about *why* you died." Because that's the next layer. The truth always comes back to soul-level agreements and intentions, love between souls so individual humans can experience all the variety of life.

Glenna: Good! I'm happy to know that because I was thinking, "Something went wrong."

Tom: Even when a person comes up to you and hates you, the souls love each other. Even if you know a person in 60,000 different lives and in every life that person slaps you in the face and tells you you're stupid – or does something really terrible – in every life it's the opportunity to learn together through experiencing all the possible varieties of human experience.

The driver of this whole thing is free will. The souls are in contract with each other – it happens within family, friendships, mate relationships, murder, and torture. One soul says, like casually in the cafeteria, "I'm looking for somebody to teach me about power. Is anybody willing to help me?" And this other soul says, "Yeah, of course! I love you. I'm going to help you learn that." The agreement gets made that when one is so-and-so – when one is Martin Luther King, Jr. – and is passionate as all get out about this message of peace and love that every time he opens his mouth he can't help but channel truth and inspire people. And that one knows it needs to learn about the ramifications in social contexts about what happens as a result. Well, sometimes people don't like to hear you! People want to shut you up sometimes. That's a soul agreement. We're like, "Murder!! Assassination!!" But the souls thank each other for the opportunity to shoot and be shot by each other. [group laughs] For real.

If we get down deep enough, every single human is dealing with the pain from some past death. Some of us are more conscious of it than others, especially those with Mars square Pluto in their charts or for me, Mars square the nodes in the 1st. We're all to some degree dealing with it. We've spent so much time in patriarchal religions where if something bad happens to you you think it because you might have not done something right to make God happy. We're all coming out of that but we're also all dealing with death. If you follow fears back enough it will come back to, "Because I believe I was killed for this." All the time. Why don't you want to speak up?

Glenna: It's multiple lifetimes.

Tom: Yeah. You don't even have to ever have been a witch, which is a really common thing in metaphysical and astrology circles. When somebody has an activated 11th house or something they might say, "I got destroyed by the mob – I was a witch." I've heard it a lot, anyway. Even if not anything like that, we've also experienced disease and illness where we feel that somebody else got us sick or we got ourselves sick, or made a stupid choice, so there's another thing about death. Why does death occur? Death occurs because your chapter's complete because your soul says, "Okay, great, done." It's not to check out to move to the next thing but maybe this chapter of learning is complete. I struggle with this. I remember dying and it fucking sucks. I remember individuals murdering me. I remember car accidents where I wasn't driving and if I had only been driving (the feeling goes) I could have prevented it. I feel all of this in my body.

One of the final frontiers for me is accepting the truth that we die at the right time even if traumatic again and again. We die at the right time. I'm still not to the place where I'm over being bullied in junior high and I'm not over all these deaths – same thing because it's about me taking responsibility for having created the experience. We all have something to work on. But it does have a lot to do with why we think death occurs and we've watched other people die. We all hear about the swim team star who's 16 who's being scouted who has a terrible car accident and dies. Or the grandmother killed by the drunk driver. We all know about these things happening. And why do these people die? Well, their souls learn through ways of dying, too, as well as ways of living.

So where are we with Glenna's chart?

Glenna: We talked a little about the North Node.

Tom: Okay, so that's where we are. Thank you. So creativity and slowing down –

Candace: Bliss.

Tom: Right, because you haven't had it before. But it's also about being heard and having your feelings be taken seriously by others. Making sure that you choose relationships in which you are honored and that you feel inspired to honor these others. So you don't have to use charm to be accepted. And the 9th house – developing a guiding principle is important, about what's worth believing in. It does have a lot to do with relationships, especially with a history of feeling betrayed or abandoned.

When I do this with people I run through this process but when somebody – like I said, if she came in to me with this chart and said she wanted to talk about her job, I'm happy to do that. But there are so many levels on which to read the chart, just like there are different levels on which to read these symbols such as Pluto as the soul's journey being squared by Mars, the South Node ruler. In my way of thinking I choose to read it in two ways, on two levels. When you're doing Pluto you're squared by Mars and when you're doing your Mars you're squared by Pluto. And they're different. But then the other layer is Sun, Moon, Rising, and the tools you have at the personality level. I notice that I spend a great deal of time focusing on the karmic symbols and the soul-level stuff because that's where I find juice first. As mentioned in *The Soul's Journey I*, I do look at the whole chart. It's just that this is where I begin because anything that you would really want to talk to me about would be related to this structure. If you come in and want to talk about your job I can look at the 10th house and the Midheaven ruler, the 6th house and the 2nd house – I can do that but behind that is going to be this karmic stuff. There is nothing that is on your heart or in your field that is not in this 4-step structure – nothing.

Glenna: What would you tell that person about her job?

Tom: I would find out what she wants to know and then I would work on discerning what's really going on. If it's a matter of one job or another I might not focus on the karma but I would think about Moon on the North Node. "Well, what makes you happier? What do you want?" And with Mars – want – quincunx Saturn in the 1st we might have to sort out what you think you should be doing versus what you want to be doing. I improv along all these possible garden paths. I basically play at getting to the real issue even if it's not what you asked about, and we can talk about it without talking about it.

Jillian: It's going to back to your soul anyway because all the elements are, all the parts of our psyche are in play. Especially in the case of a job – being in your power, shining, being your Mars as drive squaring Sun and Pluto – that line about power.

Tom: Right. Even if you don't want to hear about karma or reincarnation, I'm going to factor into every answer I give you these layers Jillian is talking about. If you don't want to hear about reincarnation, that's fine – I don't care. But I will take into account the soul's deepest wounding, here including Pluto squared by Mars and opposed by Sun in the 2nd house, the house of money and self-worth. Neptune's on the Midheaven and retrograde in Scorpio quincunx South Node ruler – what does she want? She's probably afraid to tell anybody! She may never tell me. Earlier in my career I would gently go down that road and try to coax them out: "well, I think you do know what you want. Can we talk about it? What did you want to do when you were a kid?" I would do that but now I work on seeing behind the screens and honoring that the person might not want to get into depth, especially with Pluto in the 8th like I said earlier with drawing clients who didn't want to tell me what they wanted to talk about.

Jillian: Is there a flip side with Pluto in the 8th coming and saying, "I'll tell you all!"

Tom: Recently, yeah. It might have to do with my turning a corner in comfort with delivering news that might be difficult to receive. Part of my Pluto-Venus in the 12th in Libra process – and that of the Sun in Scorpio – has been being willing to be absolutely honest when people ask me a question. Like the thing earlier about the quick fuck when Glenna was trying to open her heart. I didn't want to say that because I have Libra rising and I don't want to do that – and I know the power of words. And if I saw something, if accurate it might affect you. Not that you're not responsible for yourself and you're not a fully functioning adult, but if I'm setting out to create peace – Pluto in Libra – I want to be as gentle as possible.

Glenna: Don't you just use your intuition to see ...? I felt you energetically checking in and I gave you permission.

Tom: And that's why I did it. There are lots of times when I ... Because I have a mouth on me and I know the power words can have, and I know that words can hurt. So I think that shift in the clientele – and you're one of those 8th-house people who showed up and revealed all, so it was probably within the last two years that it started.

Glenna: It's also symbolic that you had to earn the right to enter, though. Because initially I said, "I don't know – I want you to be sure you're prepared." It was that you hadn't gotten the birth data … you'd been sick, and it was a perfect conspiracy of the Universe.

Tom: I'm glad you recognize that because at the time I thought, "This is a perfect conspiracy of the Universe and I hope she sees that."

Glenna: Yeah, it was. And then the birth date was lost and I didn't want to do it that evening because I wanted you to have more time to prepare because I'm an astrologer and I know it takes time.

Tom: But I happen to work multidimensionally.

Glenna: It was a setup for us to have to work through that.

Candace: For her to have the courage to stand up to your authority.

Glenna: I could have been intimidated by you. I needed to be able to not be in fear around it. I wanted a relationship where I could feel I could be honest and tell you what I need. So in a way it felt like the witch meeting me in the garden with a beer – we've gotten over that hump and I got the goodies. I totally got my needs met.

But there was also this element of having this hurdle to go over right at first with you. And it's nice to know from your perspective that Pluto in the 8th had been tricky and then there was this change. It makes sense to me.

Tom: It's a being willing to confront people. When you run a lot of 8th house or Scorpio energy, if you have any judgments about it whatsoever you will draw people who judge it.

Candace: Wait, say that again?

Tom: When you run a lot of Scorpio energy – Pluto, 8th house – if you have any judgments about it – *I might be too intense; I might make people uncomfortable* – you draw people you make uncomfortable. Not everyone will tell you it's too intense but you will draw people who are uncomfortable. I was uncomfortable with the idea of who was hiding out in my basements and attics. [group laughs]

Jillian: Looking behind ... looking in your closets.

Tom: Apocalyptic anger at God, life, the Universe, and every fucking person who ever gave me a problem. Such serious anger, you can't even ... And I didn't want to feel it. Well, I edged into being willing to feel it while being grounded and open to it so, essentially, feeling all that's available to feel and what's in my heart – and my other organs – but not shutting down and not running away from it. The more willing I am to confront what's ugly in myself, the more willing I am to hear what anybody is saying. If I'm judging it I draw judgment.

There have been some difficult answers I've had to provide myself on certain topics and that has opened the door to shifting how 8th-house clients come to me.

Glenna: I'm grateful for that. It felt perfect but it also felt challenging.

Tom: We also, you and I, have Saturn karma as souls, behind the scenes. And that hurdle determined whether or not you were going to be willing to work with me. I have karma of being a tyrannical authority figure – I just do. And I have it with you, too, Candace, by the way – you know that.

Candace: Really?

Tom: Do you not know that?

Candace: First time I – *second* time I was late for a session.

Tom: Oh, that's right! [group laughs] Not the first time, the second time! I think you were only late twice, right?

Candace: It was enough – for you.

Tom: That's right.

Candace: And boy! It was the last for me.

Tom: I remember that I didn't have to be caustic because you could feel what I was thinking. I didn't have to say much other than, "That doesn't work for me." Oh, did I say more? Hm, I didn't remember.

Candace: Thank you. If I can't deal with honesty, I'm a goner.

Tom: Anyway, that karma's in place separately, outside the professional relationship that you are thinking of having with me. I'll just tell you this: There are times when I draw very Jupiterian/Sagittarian people who have been indoctrinated by patriarchal religion – specifically Catholicism – and then they come to my class and their minds get blown. I have karma of spreading teachings that I don't believe in. Now I'm doing things I believe in so I'm drawing people out of the woodwork one by one – so there's that period that happens. And there's another period of Saturn people where I have the opportunity to be soft and pliable, flexible, understanding, and compassionate, which heals Saturn karma.

Candace: Bring it on, because it's juicy.

Glenna: It's so long awaited for all of us. It's all in the big pot together.

Tom: I know.

Jillian

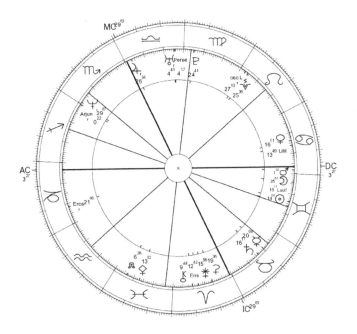

June 4, 1970, 9:29 PM, Livonia, MI

Tom: Let's go to Jillian's chart. This is the 4-step method and the first step is Pluto. Looking at the intentions and desires of the soul, the soul's empowerment journey, and the soul's wounding. It's in Virgo in the 8th and actually a degree and a half from the 9th. I know Jillian and I just don't read it in the 9th very often but we probably could. But there's a heavy emphasis on the 8th house because the South Node is also there.

With Virgo in the 8th the soul's intentions are to become empowered through intimacy and trust, which we discussed with Glenna yesterday. So we have some of the same vocabulary words though her journey is unique. Virgo is about responsibility and in the 8th house about learning for what one is really responsible within relationship. But there is also an emphasis on making choices. Becoming empowered through making choices within intimate relationship whether that's romantic, sexual, business, or friendship – or your lawyer knows all your dirty money secrets – that kind of business. The intention of the soul is to become empowered through intimate relationship but then you will have layers of debris surrounding the ability to trust and the Virgo piece about choices: what relationships to be in and how to comport the self in them is a big deal at the soul level. She points out to me that it is stationed, which means that it was slow in its motion when she was born preparing to reverse direction. How I understand that in life is that the energy is emphasized and it stands out. There's this emphasis on Plutonian energy for her because of this and it's so to speak in its own house, the 8th. How this Plutonian energy works, which is separate from the soul's mission, is highlighted within her – it's swollen, it's big – like injected with a lot of air like a balloon. All we say about her Pluto and how she might experience it has to include that perspective on the pressure happening from the inside out.

The aspects to Pluto include a square to Mars in Cancer and a square to Moon in Gemini. These squares are friction to the Plutonian mission. The soul says, "I'm going to learn about Mars in Cancer – expressing will in an emotional way – and Moon in Gemini – emotions, needs, and happiness in terms of flexibility and new information – by being in friction with them." She will at different times in all of these soul's lives draw very emotional people to her who are aggressive, assertive, or – emotional but active about it. She's learning through that. But as we explored with Glenna's square from Mars to Pluto, at times this can manifest in uncomfortable ways. The soul-level intention is to learn about it this way while she at some point is going to have to dig through the debris about what happened in human terms because of that soul's intention.

For her, unraveling karma about this particular aspect is going to involve looking at when she's been hurt by others, asking why that happened, and evaluating the assumptions that parts of her have. Because parts of her – not her if she's feeling grounded and spiritually sophisticated – will be imprinted by the emotional experiences in the past and they will then devise strategies to try to protect the self later – we all do it. So when I ask you if you have a belief about some time when you were hurt, a part of you will say, "Well, this is why it happened and I've got my eye on the details and circumstances around me to stay aware of potential repeats; so I can never let it happen again." It's about necessary and sufficient conditions: "I was hurt and here are 5 reasons it happened."

And then 35 years later a part of you finds itself able to discern 3 of those 5 conditions repeated in another scenario and the radar goes off. The parts of a person have assumptions about why things happen.

For you, Jillian, any time that you have perceived that aggressive emotional energy has hurt you – squared you and kept you from your mission – parts of you will have created beliefs and that is the stuff to unravel. I do know some of your history but if you want to give context or feedback, let's have it in terms of observing why parts of you believe that things happen and then changing things one by one.

Annette: Were these intentions set before birth?

Tom: It's happening holographically in all of these lives. This particular human is born with the emotional memories imprinted of things that are happening across the Earth timeline – it's holographic.

Annette: Wow.

Tom: Remember I talked about the veil dissolving between dimensions including the partitions in consciousness between you and your past lives? I'm not sure if I said it quite this way but one of the things to note is that it is all happening simultaneously from the emotional/energetic standpoint. Because we believe we are tied to time – we link our consciousness to time because our bodies are tied to time – a thing in for example 1250s China has already happened because of our conception of the Earth time line. Emotionally and from the soul's perspective it is all happening right now. So this woman,

202

Jillian, as a baby born already contains that and millions of other imprints. Some of them are louder than others but she contains a large number of them.

Anne: So in a way we're living all of these lives all at the same time?

Tom: From the soul's perspective, yes. Ten years ago I wouldn't have taught it this way. In another life 300 years ago I couldn't have taught it in this way. Because now we are at the place in the evolution of consciousness where we're feeling the past-life stuff so much more directly. The result is that what's on your mind isn't just what happened to you at points in this life but all of it – it's all on your mind and heart. From the point of view of the soul it's all happening simultaneously. That's why I emphasize soul so much: you're feeling it and you're living the life in 1250 rural China as well as 2,000 BCE Egypt, as well as 3,050 Idaho. You're living all of them right now. So she's born with that imprint but it happened on the Earth time line elsewhere.

Annette: Is there significance to the number 5?

Tom: No, just a random number I chose about possible variables that lead up to some hurtful scenario.

Annette: Okay. Jillian, when that wound comes up and maybe you have a little insight about where it came from, are you on a realization level that you may be facing karma from more than one life?

Jillian: Oh, yeah.

Annette: So do you get visions or insights, or do you stay connected with that wound at that time – does it sometimes take you places or does it always take you places?

Jillian: It depends. When I feel the emotions, I feel them. I'm really in touch with my personal mythology through dreams about other lives and Akashic record readings. In this life I see the symbols and in tune with the cues internally and externally. I'm not expertly realized but I think I'm good at understanding why I've drawn something to learn from it and how I've changed over time as a result.

Annette: [inaudible] or is it just healed and …?

Jillian: I just feel lighter after I go through something and clear it out, bring in God or whatever is needed.

Tom: I want to ask you when those things come up do you see the assumption or belief and then decide that that's not really happening right now and then you are relieved? Is that how works or how does it work for you when you move some of that energy?

Jillian: It's not all the time because I'm blind to certain things or not ready to heal things. In general it's like a click: I'll see the sense of experiences I'm having and get the bird's-eye view of me. I almost go into over-soul mode where I'm like, "Oh, little Jillian!" And the conscious personality part of whatever that was – it allows me to let that go and move on.

Tom: Great. This workshop's about consciously digging through the strata but all of us will have the experience of something just coming up from under the surface. Zooming out to get the bird's-eye view is, if we stay with the analogy of archaeology, how we see what it really is and label and categorize and classify it and see what we're going to do with it. That bird's-eye view is what I want everybody to gain. We're naturally swept away by the emotions so if we can, at the same time, also zoom out, we set ourselves up for progress. That's why I wanted to know how the process works for you. I know that you have at times had those kinds of experiences of gaining insight into why something is happening – imaginative and intuitive.

Jillian: Like the conversation we were having this morning. Maybe months ago or if it was with someone else, you stated a need this morning or had a request about how future interactions go regarding some particular thing. In the past because it would have pushed older buttons and I could have responded differently. I might have been like, "nooo!!" [group laughs] With Mars square Pluto part of me would want control of that kind of thing. Over time I've been able to recognize those buttons for what they are and not push them.

Tom: Good. I want to talk about control with you. It could apply somewhat to Glenna, too, though her Mars square Pluto is from the 5th house and Jillian's is from the 6th. But each to Pluto in Virgo and control is a key word for Virgo. I want to talk about that as an evolutionary response to feeling out of control because something's coming at you from the side. So you have a response and now have to ask, "What is control, really?" So asking any of you except for the moment Jillian, what is control about?

Candace: Ideally, self-empowerment.

Tom: Okay. But what does it look like? What do parts of you assume control should look like?

Candace: Ooh.

Tom: Yeah – I want to do this for a second because it's a great exercise.

Glenna: For me it's brakes on a car and my steering wheel.

Tom: Okay, good. And where does that get you?

Glenna: And I can go anywhere I want with it.

Summer: Control for me might be feeling grounded and stable. Having an agenda.

Tom: What would that get you? What would being like that lead to?

Summer: Accomplishment.

Tom: Okay, good. I just want to look at some of the assumptions that parts of us have and whether they're our savvy minds or presumptive inner parts. I want to hear a variety of things.

Candace: We don't want to be embarrassed! [group laughs]

Tom: Great!

Michael: When I feel control I don't worry about my balance. I just know that I have it. That's my feeling of control.

Tom: And what does it feel like when you're not centered?

Michael: Scattered. Don't have the brakes on anything.

Tom: And where does that lead?

Michael: Loose ends back in.

Tom: Jillian, since you're the one who brought up the word control, I'm vibing on your sense of it.

Jillian: Let me preface it by drawing attention to the fact that my Sun, Moon, and Mars are all in the 6th house and the Virgo perfectionism part of it.

Tom: Understood.

Jillian: For me, control is intrinsically wrapped up in paying attention to every detail, loving every detail, too. It's wrapped up with creation. If I were a god and created a galaxy or something I would want to have control over putting my attention and love into every detail because I want it to be perfect. It's like, just like with you, controlling your energies – what you create and how you manifest.

Tom: Thank you. So Pluto in Virgo has an intention to learn how to control. But with Mars-Moon square it from the 6th and Pluto being stationed – standing still – the need for control can get augmented and the strategies of how it can happen and how to make sure it happens can get numerous and intense. Mars-Moon square the soul's mission can be chaos – emotional chaos coming to you. I wanted to point out to Jillian but wanted to involve as many people as possible that the Pluto in Virgo already tries to control but emotional chaos coming your way makes you develop even more strategies and put even more pressure on yourself to stay in control. Emotional archaeology for you regarding this Pluto – I know I'm really focusing on this aspect and we will go on to do the whole chart, but I really wanted to get into this in part because Glenna had a similar thing; this is the next level of conversation about this Pluto setup and Glenna didn't use the word control but Jillian did. There's a potential for you to overwork to be in control but the spiritual truth is that there is no such thing as control. Especially as with Pluto in the 8th you are intending to learn through intimate partnership and there's no such thing as control when you're dealing with others intimately. To try to control is an adaptive thing to protect yourself and your soul's mission. Emotional archaeology for you would be to look at why you think control is needed. On the personality level yes, Sun, Moon, and Mars are in the 6th, great. But underneath that, Sun and Moon are ways to develop tools but the fact is that you might overwork. So the digging down for you is looking at the assumptions about why control is necessary and then going through each instance in your life when you have felt either that you didn't have control and should have or you did but didn't do it right or enough, and changing the meanings attached to those files. I do want to move on but wanted to get through that.

Michael: Thank you for that – it was really helpful. Looking at that notion – when it is and isn't, when it could be – and then that in the soul's deepest place, control isn't necessary.

Tom: Good. I was talking earlier about the soul-level intention of Pluto in Scorpio of being intense but then having to deal with the repercussions of choices of intensity. The soul-level intention with the Pluto in Virgo is to improve something but then you have to get to the place where you understand what really can be improved, like the Desiderata: Grant me the blah blah blah. What really can be improved but then what really should be improved. It's kind of like dealing with the debris that's layered over the core intention. So, being available to make something better leaves it open ended – "I'm available to help somebody." How different that is with Pluto in Virgo energy.

Candace: Wow.

Glenna: Do you feel that it's almost a square of Virgo to Virgo with all that energy? The commitment to all this quality, precision craftsmanship in this lifetime – this really intense precision reflected even in this decision to come just one minute before Pluto went direct. [group laughs] "Okay, you ready?! I'm here – okay – go go!!" Even in that but yet the call of the soul saying, "Okay, but you gotta let go and you're gonna learn this through other people."

Tom: Exactly! And you're going to encounter others who won't let you control things. That's the conversation this morning. She kind of, in the spirit of wanting something to be good and helping me she made an assumption, but I'm a 2nd-house Sun – I will not let anybody control anything! [group laughs]

Glenna: That's interesting that you attracted him.

Tom: I will come to the table to negotiate.

Jillian: And it's *Scorpio* in the 2nd.

Tom: That's the emotional archaeology to be done on Pluto. I've never seen it that way with you but as soon as you said "control" all these crumpled-up pieces of paper constellated in my mind [group laughs] and I got it.

Annette: I'm glad you didn't ask me about control! [group laughs] I'm spazzing out over here.

Candace: So am I!

Tom: Are you? Well, it's actually a normal, natural human thing. The desire to protect ourselves. The desire to be the agent of change in our lives instead of feeling that we're at the mercy and whim of everything. You know, we don't have anybody with Pluto in Pisces on the planet right now but we have people with Pluto in the 12th house. To contrast it, their intention of the soul is to learn to surrender. Well, what's going to happen? They're going to have human experiences where they actually do surrender and then they say, "Well, that hurts! Control!!" [group laughs] So then you're going to have people with Pluto in the 11th or Aquarius and they're going to have the soul-level intention to learn to fit into a group. Well, what happens when you fit into a group? Sometimes you get trampled by a mob and they end up trying this, "I have to control my participation in a group!" attitude. And then everyone else – control is a natural response to getting hurt.

Candace: Instinctive response.

Tom: Yes.

Candace: Instinctive survival response.

Tom: Because we perceive ourselves to be separate and then we experience ourselves to be separate. I don't know if I mentioned it yesterday or not but one thing I'm working with now is dealing with ways I've died in various lives. I'm mad – I'm like, "Somebody needs to do something this because I can't deal with that anymore! That can't happen again!" But if I learn to trust it, then what comes up is a question about getting done what I need to get done – that's a thing from other lives, that there isn't enough time because I died young or whatever. So of course I will strive to control but my Pluto in the 12th says that I need to fit in to the big picture and accept the real reasons why things happen. With Candace we talked about the adaptive response with the weather event she couldn't control – that's my future. [sighs out slow and long] Relaxing into the flow of things. Candace's future is getting more proactive. Mine is the opposite. But the point is that the control thing is relevant to every single one of us.

The second step here is Jillian's South Node, in Virgo in the 8th. There are echoes here – picking families and conditioning environments in many lives that reflect the same kind of energy that the soul-level intention of Pluto in Virgo in the 8th has. She's going to pick families where there are boundary issues because the 8th is where we learn to merge or we accidentally get entangled. There are also going to be issues about responsibility and self-control as well as controlling others. And there are going to be issues about truth and trust. It's in common because Pluto is in the same sign as her South Node – not everybody has that. I'm going to pull in the conjunction to the true Black Moon Lilith at 27 Leo, also in the 8th. The Vesta is for me a degree too wide but it's bought in by implication because of the conjunction to Lilith. Vesta-Lilith in Leo in the 8th – there is such an incredible emphasis on being honest in a natural, open, flowing way ... or blocking it because it brings up too much hard stuff. She's going to have some lives where she picks a family in which everyone is an exemplar of telling difficult truths from a place of love versus not talking about anything today or this decade. [group laughs] It will be back and forth – she'll have memories of needing that honesty and being born to families that can't do it and she'll also have memories of being born into families in which she has to hold something back because everyone else is so intense and honest that she just needs some private time once in a while: *I don't need you to look into my heart all the time.* So we know those extremes about her family system and karmic history in many lives.

Square the South Node is Neptune in late Scorpio and Arjunsuri in early Sagittarius, and these are in the 11th. Again, squares to the nodes I treat as unresolved issues. The person knows many things about the energy but not enough to feel happy, successful, or healthy. It's a tripping over your shoe laces or sticking your foot in your mouth. Neptune is about how we connect to other realities, how we bring the Divine into daily life, and how we approach meditation, mysticism, art, and creativity. Arjunsuri is about conscience and our relationship with our own inner wisdom. With Neptune in Scorpio and Arjunsuri in Sagittarius here, there's an issue about belief and power through belief – becoming empowered through maintaining one's own belief. Each of these is retrograde so she's going to in many lives spend time that might seem wasted pursuing Neptunian things – certain forms of truth that in the end turn out to be flotsam and jetsam or not real/not true. She's got some karmic history of seeking truth and having it turn out to be not quite what it seemed in the beginning.

The other square to the nodes is the Sun-Lucifer conjunction in the 6th house. Sun is the biggest thing in the personality – the biggest thing in the solar system and therefore the biggest thing within us. I think of it as the inner CEO. There's a meeting where these couple dozen energies are talking. The Sun should be the one who's running the show and when the Sun is square the nodes, there's an issue with developing a healthy ego. Sun is one of the markers we can look at to determine how a person might try to control things – running the meeting in the psyche. So there's an unresolved issue with what ego looks like. It's in the 6th house so it becomes a question about how she can develop a healthy ego through service, being useful to others in some way, providing or fulfilling a useful function. On the personality level her sanity depends on doing it but on the karmic level underneath that it's confusing because she's made choices A and B thousands of times and, in the end, saw that neither option really worked. Perhaps she thinks C and D are terrible choices and so hasn't explored them, maybe in time she does and they don't work out either but A and B still don't work. So it's that there's this karmic confusion: she knows something about it but it doesn't work and she doesn't know the other thing but she doesn't think that's going to work, either.

Adding Lucifer in it furthers the idea of healthy ego and about being willing to shine. Conjunct the Sun, this entire existential project is wrapped up in learning how to shine, learning how to express the self in a healthy way. One of the things about the Lucifer story, which is told in *Living Myth* – well first, forget the Christian mythos about the devil, Satan, and evil. That's just the name of the asteroid. We have to back to the Hebrew version of the same exact story of the fallen archangel, whose name is Samael. According to the Bible's Genesis business, when God creates Adam God calls all the angels together and says, "Look what I made – this is the greatest creation next to me. Please bow down before this wonderful creation that is second only to me in gloriousness." Two-thirds of the angels naturally go, "Oh, great! Yeah! God's so cool!" And Samael says, "Wait a minute – you told us we that we were your Divine essence and we represent your Divinity out there, and now you're wanting us to bow down before a being made of dirt. I just don't know about that." And God says, "Just do it." It's the patriarchal god, right? "This is the game plan." Samael says, "I love you too much to let you act like an idiot, to go against yourself and act out of integrity. So I can't stay here because I can't support you right now though I love you dearly." In the Lucifer story in the Christian mythos, it's about evil and badness and breaking away from and working against God. Forget that because that's a way of demonizing doubt so that we'll all just go along and do the patriarchal agenda. But the original story has to do with integrity.

It becomes, "So this archangel thinks he's better than God?!" Shining. How can you have the arrogance? Lucifer-Sun people – and actually Glenna, Jillian, and I are Lucifer-Sun people – if you really shine people might want to call you arrogant because they're not sure if they should let you try to be bigger than God. It's about healthy ego.

But conjunct the Sun and square the nodes – specifically in that context – there is this thing about being afraid of shining too much but that leads to avoiding developing a healthy ego, so that's a major issue. The unresolved issue is how much can she shine, how much service can she really offer of the kind that feels best to her, without being arrogant and egotistical?

Because we're talking about squares to the nodes we're talking about her family system as well – people trying to figure out the right way to have a healthy ego. There are going to be people in her family whose egos are in the toilet and others who are in the stratosphere. Because the family system is learning about this and it fits her karma, her journey.

And then conjunct the North Node, the last bit for step 2, is the asteroid Pallas Athene, who is also represented in *Living Myth*. There are different threads I work with when looking at this archetype. One is a part of us that we try to divorce ourselves from because we're more successful if we don't show up as that. It's that people around us are uncomfortable about it so we'd just rather keep it quiet – we're more successful if we just kind of go with the program. But it's also about protection, sponsoring others in a protective way – like I'm looking out for you, so there's a warrior energy here – and there's also an issue about loyalty with Pallas Athene. Conjunct the 2nd house North Node, in her family system and in her karmic history loyalty to one's own value system is sacrificed in order to live in the 8th house of entanglement. "I'm aware of what you're feeling and we're wrapped up together even if we're not talking about it." You being committed to being a self-esteem warrior gets left out, but also in your family system so they couldn't teach you how to believe in yourself and how to stand up for yourself as a love warrior – they couldn't teach you.

Step 3 is the South Node ruler. This is Mercury because Mercury rules Virgo and so we go straight to the end of the 4th house. I think some people have read it in the 5th for you and we could do that but it's conjunct Saturn in the 4th and I wonder if it's pulled back and so more relevant being read in the 4th. She shows up in this family system of Virgo/8th-house stuff – the desire to be together but also the entanglement that can result, with me not being sure where you end and where I begin –and she is a Taurus Saturn-4th house figure. Living in the 4th house is being in touch with the inner world. Adding Saturn to that there's this need to be autonomous and competent. In Taurus it's trying to slow down. In the chaos of whatever place she finds herself in that fits the South Node, she is trying desperately to figure out how to disentangle from it and slow down so she can have a center of gravity that's just hers. I know that about you and you know that about you but in the context of this story, I want to point out that it's multilife thing: surrounded by chaos and emotional things being thrown at you and you're just like, "I just need 10 minutes alone." But those 10 minutes are repeated billions of times over millions of years.

In this process of emotional archaeology and digging down through the strata, you should just know that regularly doing that without inspiration is important. Like a daily meditation practice.

Jillian: Right.

Tom: Where you don't ever get to the point where the little light goes off on the meter that says, "now I need to have 20 minutes by myself." It's been a response but it needs to be a foundational, daily thing.

Jillian: Right.

Tom: That's what I want to do with that. Let's go to the North Node.

Jillian: Could you speak to – oh, I guess that's it: my preferred role is to slow down and meditate.

Tom: You show up as the person who needs that. Maybe not meditate but to have your own space. But you're in this 8th-house chaotic environment where everyone's entangled.

Jillian: Right.

Tom: But you show up as somebody with a different set of values, too. Taurus and Saturn – you're going to show up with some conservatism and an interest in consolidating energy instead of trying to control everything. That's actually your role but when you try to control things it's because of the environment you're in.

Candace: Because it's so chaotic.

Tom: Yes and you need to have to control over yourself. That Taurus energy wants to hunker down and send cords into the Earth and be like, "This is my little castle that I live in – this is my stone tower that can't be moved." But in the context of chaos in the environment it can be hard to do.

The North Node in Pisces in the 2nd house – surrendering to your own needs. Surrendering to your own value system, what is most important to you. I say surrender but it's allowing yourself to flow with what is most important to you. You'll know what's most important to you but if I or someone else asks you might not have an answer right away because if you're focused on, distracted by, or wrapped up in 8th-house chaos you might not be clear. Like when you were 15 if someone asked you what was most important to you you would have responded with what someone else wanted you to think was most important because you've been so strongly conditioned that way. In maturity of course you can grow into that. You also need to have faith that what is most important to you is actually important – that's this North Node. Looking at the 8th house context to contrast this, every time there is an interaction that is important to her, she's got to remember where she is in the dialogue and not see it as a see-saw just going back and forth but that she is sitting on one end of a see-saw and it can be worked. Not just automatically, "I want what you want" – can't do that anymore.

Glenna: I wonder if there's anything you're willing to share, insights you have around that karma, feeling the 8th-house chaos and coming to need to be true to yourself.

Jillian: A lot of it is about that Sun-Lucifer conjunction, and the squares to Pluto. 8th house South Node in Virgo is like being submerged into the 8th house and not knowing where I end and you begin – the boundaries thing. So I don't know where I end and you begin and if I'm in this dark Pluto/8th-house place I can't find my light, really difficult to find it and to shine and express myself.

Audience: Do you find it difficult to be the authority in your life?

Jillian: Definitely. I find myself trying out all these things that other people – trying on religions, trying on clothes, whatever – trying on jobs, occupation.

Candace: What feels good?

Jillian: What feels good?

Candace: What part of you can let yourself go, "When I let myself go into an expansive sense of feeling … where I can just surrender to my bliss, which is my skill and my talent?" Do you have any part of you that goes instantly to that kind of place?

Jillian: A little bit with music and words.

Candace: That's what I wanted to hear. The bliss of oneness. "Where I just have to show up and bring my music, bring my Neptunian part that says, 'Can we just get together around the fire, and can we just do a radio program?' Can we talk about these things that I love?"

Jillian: Exactly.

Candace: That you would be in control of? That *you* pick what you want on it.

Tom: But I want to point out a blind spot about control. It might look like you would be in control but being participatory in an active way is different than being in control of something. I don't want you ever to think you need to be in control of something. That's what it looks like it should be like but it's –

Candace: It doesn't have that kind of form.

Tom: Right. "I want to play with you this way – do you want to play with me that way? Great – let's play together."

Candace: That's what happened around the fire last night. It was sort of flowy, spontaneity, everyone just sort of participated and then everybody got a little more comfortable participating.

Jillian: I have to tell you I recorded a little bit of that last night and I listened to it as I was falling asleep. I completely picked myself apart for trying to direct everything, trying to control everyone. It was good for me to record that so I could hear myself doing that because I don't find that too attractive. And to learn a little bit of the grace and to let go.

Candace: But did you record the later part, when everybody did just let go? Surrender?

Jillian: Ohh.

Glenna: I'm having a knot in my stomach about something and it hurts in my head, too. So there might be a mental energy block around it. Everyone needs a gas pedal and brakes and a steering wheel. There's an element of the autonomy that it seems that this soul has come to get about control, so not shaming it – I understand what you're saying about control, but it seems like don't throw the baby out with the bathwater. Not all or nothing.

Tom: Can I say something about the conversation we had? I said, "I really need there not to be any assumptions about this thing, but come to me and we'll discuss and we'll make a decision together. When I find the assumption I just kind of shut down – I don't do that." That might look to some of us like she has no control over it but what's actually happening is she'll get her way in that conversation half the time when we have it down the road.

This idea of control stirs something in us anyway.

Glenna: It does. [group laughs]

Tom: When you do seek to have equality about something – and here we're talking about a business arrangement – then she'll say, "This is how I want it to be done." There are certain things I have a strong stance on and there are other things that I am happy to shift about.

Glenna: You're talking about honoring your needs – maybe that puts it in a more comfortable context for me because there's a certain tyrannical feeling –

Candace: "LET GO OF CONTROL."

Glenna: I'm feeling that in my arms, too. It's like, "ooh, I'm not good with that." I want to grab the steering wheel and it's not because I want to run you over. [group laughs]

Tom: You don't want to feel swept away or out of control?

Glenna: I want to drive with you and I want to honor my own needs for the kind of car I want to be in, but I'm not okay with anyone just driving up and kind of rumbling right over me either – anymore. I think I probably have been in the past.

So the distinction between "you get the dignity of owning your own need" and not making it about – there's something in me that reacts to almost feeling shamed about just taking up space, which I know I'm learning.

Candace: Must be Pisces because I feel the same way.

Tom: Pluto in the 8th – shamed about taking up space. Because you're going to draw people to you who have the effect of overpowering you because you're learning about power within intimate relationships and with people who are energetically big. You each draw this Scorpio with Pluto conjunct Venus in the 12th – yet you test the waters: How much of a right do I have to take up space? And I tell you I want you to be my equal and we should negotiate. But I bring such a forceful personality that part of you gets triggered.

Jillian: The funky irony is that I'm so Virgo-oriented to serve and end up in the background, and my lesson is about Saturn in a sense: taking up physical space and meditating, and having my own authority.

Tom: But for your own reasons and not as a reaction against other people who seem more powerful.

Jillian: Right!

Tom: That's the archaeology here. Because everything that you react to about me is not about me. It's about your buttons – same with Glenna, same with Candace. It's a similar kind of Saturnian dynamic that I trigger in each of you.

Candace: It triggers invisibility, the need to take up space.

Tom: I'm not trying to make this about me but I'm observing these tendrils –

Candace: Thanks!

Tom: Because I've worked with each of you as clients and I consider each of you a friend, so I have this dual perspective and also the karmic perspective.

Candace: We're all Pluto/8th house – we've all got Pluto/8th house issues. About entanglement with power and where we've given it away.

Tom: I show up as somebody who is really clear about what he wants. But I also demand that you also get clear about what you want – and I will ask you!

Glenna: We attracted you for that reason.

Tom: My Pluto-in-Libra thing needs to have equality. I might not know how to do it all the time and there are things I won't budge on, but I want to know what you think.

What I want to get at here is the idea of reacting from the past versus being present and recognizing the button.

When specifically you, Glenna, tell me what you want, it might challenge me, but –

Glenna: And I can feel that, at least in my experience, arrive to you and maybe you weren't too happy about it. But it's okay. It's new, but good. There's more in that that I'm being called to challenge myself courageously to own my truth. Kind of like what you told me about these guys: "Go ahead and allow them to have their experience." So I can allow you to have your reaction and not feel like I'm going to get shot now. It's a karmic thing. The last time I spoke my truth like that, honey, I got run through right through the kidney. Somebody just came up behind me and said, "Just get rid of her!" Or, "off with her head!" That's what it feels like in myself when you do that.

Tom: Right.

Glenna: The more I do it with this empathetic sense even if you do react a little, it doesn't mean the same thing. And we can feel the energy somehow, because it's big energy.

Candace: It's about power and about being able to be empowered. Asking do we have the right?

Glenna: I felt it in Africa with [name inaudible] because he says, "This is a democracy" – that's the circus. But really if you say anything even through peaceful protest you get tear gassed or shot, even if you're a woman walking peacefully down the street.

Candace: Whoa.

Glenna: So I got to experience that in Africa, the feeling of that. I'm not okay with that anymore but I also don't believe in overpowering. I believe that we can listen to each other and get it all out. Sometimes you have to agree to disagree, and that's fine. But I have to be true to my own sense of things, that feeling in my kidney. [laughs]

Jillian: I want to share something about that because this whole Lucifer-Sun thing square my nodes, about speaking up and the past-life issues in there. I've examined them from lots of different angles and I feel things in my bones but among my past lives I've been a slave, a black slave sexually abused. In one Akashic record reading the reader saw me attempting to flee via the Underground Railroad across the border to Niagara Falls. It was at the time when they had these posters that said, "$50 for shooting a black person" or whatever it was.

Glenna: Oh my.

Jillian: As I was attempting to flee I was shot in the back and killed. So I've had at different stages of my life bouts of agoraphobia, fear of making too much noise, fear of being seen in public places – let alone speaking up when I go out. With the Saturn constricting my Mercury in Taurus – feeling like I can't speak – because I can't shine because I can't –

Glenn: "I'm just a farmer – who am I to speak? I'm just a land worker."

Jillian: Right. I have Chiron in Aries in the 3rd and it's accentuated when I'm in a public place when I get really nervous around other people and I've had to work on that and massage that so I can be with other people in a healthy fashion and not feel like I will be persecuted or shot. I do feel that level of anxiety – it's life or death.

Candace: And it seems to me – two things that intuitively stand out for me that are your benefits. The Taurus – the slowness. And I loved hearing what he was saying because here she is on the Taurusy piece of property, to know that that is the kind of thing that soothes your inner Mercury. The mind gets to slow down into the animal energy of calm and safe. And the Pisces says, "I get to surrender to what I love to do." If I were going to do your chart I'd say, "You spend some time on Taurus and Pisces and absorb the energies." That's what I would do.

Jillian: Actually, the North Node in the 2nd house.

Candace: Yeah, the hyper punishment, the hyper fear of "I'm gonna lose my life." Well, this lifetime it's about gentle, surrender to your values – what you love and have Enchanting Experience Radio,[16] "and here we are folks, my name is Jillian." [group laughs] "I think it's time for us to take a gentle journey down the Nile and it's not about denial." [group laughs] Whatever you could to slow and smooth and just be able to surrender to the flow of your imagination in the most protected and safe and – "I just don't have to control anything because look at me! I am so awesome." [group laughs] Can't you see yourself going there?

---

[16] Candace's healing service business, centered on the property, is called The Enchanting Experience.

Annette: And I don't understand this control thing anyway! That's a lot better way to go!

Glenna: And I can control it if I want to but it's not … in terms of "I can take it where I want it to go." Can we heal the control wounds and then come back to a gentle way – I feel that hands-on-the-steering-wheel, white-knuckled type of control versus the country drive looking here and there -- intentional. There's no shame in that.

Tom: This is all about helping us understand how we're wired and our experiences – otherwise it's just jargon.

Candace: And confusing, and complicated.

Michael: The new astrology books just have new pictures, bigger pictures, and bigger words. [group laughs] Bigger pictures and they're so confusing – there's a billion references to that sign with the little symbols, and I get kind of lost.

Tom: Let's talk about how we live.

Candace: Relating it to present-day, energetic happenings.

Tom: Right.

Anne

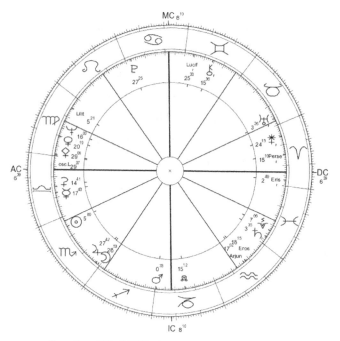

October 29, 1935, 4:10 AM, Yakima, WA

Tom: Let's do Anne's chart next. She is the person in the room who has Pluto in Cancer. We talked yesterday afternoon about some of the context of the journey with Pluto in Cancer. It's in the 10th house and does have aspects that we will talk about.

So this 1st step with Pluto – the soul intends to become empowered through living in the 10th house, which is a house of public self. It's often thought of to be about career but it's really about who you want to be in the world whether or not your job or career reflects it or not. It can be our place in the community instead of an actual career but it's your public face – that's the big thing. Through the lens of Cancer, to develop a role that allows you to show your heart or your inclination to serve, heal, help, shepherd people – something like this.

This basic intention of the soul with Pluto in Cancer is to become empowered through dealing with emotions – to become empowered through feeling. And learning about the ups and downs and nooks and crannies of a human's emotional makeup. So this is what can empower or disempower Anne and yet this is in a public context. In different lives she will have the experience of having her emotions revealed publicly – intentionally or unintentionally – that affect her reputation in her community or at her job. So this is a public display of emotion whether she means it or not. In some lives, something happens and your heart is visible and everyone can see you. It doesn't mean they judge or don't judge – we don't know that – but you're seen as an emotional person in public.

That's the fundamental, basic soul's journey. The layers, the strata of stuff to dig through with the emotional archaeology is, "Why would that happen?" Well, the soul's intention is to bring heart into the community. Another angle on this is to develop a public way of being that includes emotion. What do you do for a living? What's your thing?

Anne: I'm an artist.

Tom: Painter? Sculptor? Textiles? What is it that you do?

Anne: Yes. Drawing, painting, sculpture, clay, glass – you name it.

Tom: So people seeing the result of your emotional process?

Anne: If they want to see it.

Tom: Right, and some of them will see the product and not the process and that's fine, too. But it's available.

Michael: Through art you can't hide your heart. An art piece is right in front of everyone.

Anne: It's all there. My whole story is all there.

Glenna: May I ask if it feels intense to you? The art – is it an intense expression?

Anne: During the time I made it, before I was able to look at it from a different place and see that I was indeed telling my own story. I realize now how healing it was.

Jillian: Are there certain themes that are across all of the media?

Annette: I asked Anne if she was open to sharing it. Then I was at her house, looking at all the wonderful, different art on the wall and all of a sudden there's these sculptures – all different types of things and they all have a message, and they're very beautiful. And they're made with textiles, things from the Earth, rocks, and pieces of this and that. There's one that she brings out and shares an important story about her history, which I won't share now, but yes, that's how intense and how much of a structure there is in that art.

Tom: In other lives along the Earth timeline – we would usually say past lives – the need is to develop a public self but some or all of the institutions and people you encounter will tell you, "You can't express yourself here." That's why that's so healing. I'm touched – I'm happy to hear that that's what you do – have done and do. Having Pluto in the 10th means that in all these lives you're dealing with social expectations as well.

Anne: I went back to school as an adult and got my degree in fine arts, and at the time when I started creating that art, I thought that my intention was to make statements – social and political statements. Pretty soon I realized they were statements about my inner being. What I thought was an environmental statement was also about me. It was all about my internal landscape. I did one charcoal drawing of a polluted river and signs of industry in the background and a woman sitting in this dry river bed, looking very sad. I thought that it was just an environmental statement but it was also about my internal landscape, my internal environment.

You mentioned the public. I just recently volunteered to teach art classes to the women who are in the domestic violence program.

Jillian: That is so Cancer in the 10th! [group laughs]

Anne: Because I know that art can be a humane tool.

Tom: Ultimately, one of the byproducts of this journey for you is to become a symbol of working with emotion. It's one of the things that happens with this symbol. I'm not saying that you have crossed the finish line and you don't have to incarnate anymore but that indicates the progression of karmic healing. I'd like to ask you some questions about stuff that was going on earlier in your life relative to being an artist or you being available to be seen. This is a real progression that you're at the end of and the chapters of that story over the course of your life about who you are in public and how you understand your feelings and share or show them – all of that indicates the compression of a bunch of different lives that you will have processed and gone through. Pluto in Cancer is also a marker of becoming empowered through family connections, so when you were young, was there an expectation of what you might do when you grew up?

Anne: Within myself?

Tom: Within your family – I want to start there.

Anne: It was only within myself.

Tom: Ahh, there was no expectation.

Anne: Actually I grew up on an apple orchard not far from here, and I was about 7 years old when I started wondering what life was all about. I was drawing and I wrote poems and stories. I would look out over the wheat fields and the Cascades to the West and I would wonder what was over those mountains and thought, "Someday I want to go over and find out." So I have this spirit of adventure.

But all of this was internal because in my family no one talked about anything real ever. Not only were you not supposed to talk about anything real, you weren't even supposed to feel anything real.

Tom: Got it.

Anne: So I lived in my imagination.

Tom: We'll go there too because this chart speaks that in several different ways. But the basic Pluto idea here is the soul's intention to develop some kind of public self but maybe in some lives it not happening or not being authentic, that kind of thing. You've gone through this progression of going back to school to do the thing that you want – you're kind of there in a good way.

Now I want to talk about the squares to Pluto. We have retrograde Uranus in Taurus in the 8th. Lots of people your age are going to have this square because these are two slow-moving planets but that doesn't make it impersonal because this is squaring the marker of the soul's empowerment journey. The energy of Taurus in the 8th given a family that doesn't really talk about anything deep – this is part of it – Taurus in the 8th might want to shy away from complexity because 8th-house matters, which have to do with where we merge or get entangled with each other; are approached through Taurus. Maybe there's a conservatism or resistance or stubbornness to that. But with Uranus squaring the Pluto, your soul's mission can be derailed by sudden change from within relationships. In some lives commitments you make in relationship have kept you from developing a public self. In this life you would have had relationships that threatened to do that and they probably went away and then you would have felt open. Or is there something about relationships ending in order for you to open up to do what you want?

Anne: Oh yes. With my marriage. I knew that I absolutely needed to find out who I really am.

Tom: When you married, when you made that commitment, you weren't totally sure who you were or how it would come out, but it's also that you literally were a different person and you were a Taurean person when you made that commitment. Kind of conservative and dealing with the face value of it, the surface of it – it's static.

Anne: I tried to fit in and it was a loss. [laughs]

Tom: Yeah, it's not going to work. Because then we're going to talk about the other square to the nodes which is Sun is Scorpio in the 2nd. The soul's mission of doing something well and being recognized for it and ultimately becoming a symbol offering something from the heart – the Cancerian stuff – is squared by a Scorpio Sun in the 2nd house. Personality-wise you have a Scorpio Sun in the 2nd – that's one thing. But being squared by that energy karmically is a separate story. Your biggest tool right now – I mean in this life with the Sun – is to have the impulse to get grounded and stable and to be self-reliant but in the karmic past you've been pressed and knocked over by people like that – big personalities who are very confident, much more confident than you think you might be, pushing you. Of course the evolutionary intention is to learn about being the Sun, which is shining and being bold and big, through being pressed by it, through receiving friction from it. Does that makes sense?

Anne: No, not really.

Tom: Okay. There's an evolutionary intention to learn about Sun – boldness, creativity, shining – through being pressured by people who are very stubborn and set in their ways who represent that energy. Big personalities who might not be able to see you yet try to tell you who you are. But they might not see you.

Anne: Well, I felt invisible for a large part of my life because my feelings were never validated.

Tom: Exactly.

Anne: I finally came to the truth in the last two years that I was sexually abused by my father when I was very young. I spent all these years in relationships not understanding why but having a terrible struggle.

Tom: So these other people bring a big, intense Scorpio energy that brings friction to you. Abuse is one of the ways that squares can manifest because squares represent energies coming at you from the side and perhaps hurting you. It can also be a surprise or a differing opinion that challenges you but lots of times when we're not conscious – remember that for millions of years we've been creating through ignorance – abuse is one of the ways that that can manifest.

Digging through these layers of karma for you – the emotional archaeology – is about why those intense people have come into your life – the meanings that parts of you might have assigned When you can – and perhaps you're there now – say, "I drew these strong personalities that brought friction to me because I'm learning about how to become a strong personality and I need pressure to learn it." Basically, if they push on you, eventually you realize that your feelings need to be validated and then you do it yourself. So they are the teachers for you who are pushing you in uncomfortable ways. When you get to that place, then you change the file label on why anything happened in all those various relationships. You see that, right? That's the digging through the layers for you. You said it: "My feelings were never validated." Right! Because your soul said, "As a human, I need to learn how to do that myself."

Anne: I didn't have a clue as to what any of my feelings were.

Tom: Right.

Anne: The first time I went to a therapist and he would ask a question in my mind all I was thinking was, "What's the right answer? What does he expect me to say?" I didn't have a clue! I couldn't tell him how I felt about anything.

Summer: That's what you do through your art.

Tom: Her evolutionary path has taken her to expression but she had to find out what she felt first. We're going to get there with the nodes because that's a big deal, too. But the square to Pluto is that pressure that eventually you can learn to be a solar person in the 2nd house: "This is what I value. This is what's important to me. Here's my statement. Here's how I validate my feelings."

Anne: That's where I am now. [group claps]

Tom: Good! That's the Pluto component. Now we move on to the 2nd step of the South Node of the Moon, and we have an echo because the South Node of the Moon is Cancer in the 10th house. Earlier in life you didn't quite

236

know what your feelings were and you came from people who didn't talk about feelings, the emotional component of your family system has to do with what's happening in the world. *It's not who we are, what we're feeling, what you, child, need right now.* There can be an impersonal involvement with feelings with this Cancer South Node in the 10th. It could be a hyperelevated relationship with feelings or it could be more dampened or suppressed or left out.

Michael: Did you say impersonal?

Tom: Yes. There could be a disconnect from emotions or a real heightened experience of emotion in the family system. Like in my family, with my Cancer South Node in the 10th, a heightened experience of emotions. But in yours it's dampened – it's just different ways of learning about Cancerian energy.

One square to the nodes is Mercury-Ceres in Libra in the 1st. Ceres is about nurturing, asking oneself what one needs, and asking others, but it's about taking care of self and other. Mercury is about communication as well as conscious awareness and perceiving. I'm leaving out the sign and house for a moment but just those two symbols square the nodes say that there is an unresolved issue about what people need – you and your family. There's a way of observing practical things: "She needs a new pair of shoes." That's a valid need, right? "School's starting, these old shoes have holes – let's get her a new pair of shoes." There's a valid need but it's not the same as, "Wow, she really needs to tell us what she wants to do tomorrow. She really needs to tell us what her perfect birthday party would be like." You might need to communicate that but they might not get it.

Left out in a lot of your family karma is an awareness of how to directly – 1st house – address our needs individually and together – that's the Libra component. It's not even being sure what we really need. Then the therapist asks you what you feel and you're not quite sure what the right answer is. Well, the chart says that running through your physical body is an awareness of need. If you got into the practice of scanning your body – and maybe you do something like this – you would find questions and requests at different places in your body because you're carrying the energy of Mercury-Ceres: communicating need in your physical body. Planets in the 1st house we tend to carry unconsciously. But that's part of the thing – we don't know always know it until somebody else reflects it to us. We just carry it. My Mars-Uranus has me move and talk really fast – and I need people to ask me to slow down once in a while. I'm just not aware of it. For Anne, you needed to learn more about this because as the conjunction is square the nodes, it has been an unresolved issue in many lives. Learning more involves looking at how your family did that part of life and choosing to make different choices – the key to changing all karma.

The asteroids Persephone and Juno in Aries are also square the nodes in the 7th. With a 9-degree orb we might not consider them conjunct but each is square the nodes, and each is retrograde. Let's start with Juno – an

238

unresolved issue about the right reasons and ways to make commitments in relationship. It can look like a karmic setup to need to get married to somebody it will appear later that you shouldn't be married to in order to figure out the importance of when you make a commitment and how it affects your life, which is what you said earlier about that relationship. Have you been married more than once?

Anne: The second time for a very period of time. I've had a couple of other long-term relationships – all disasters.

Tom: Why you choose them is the thing. This is actually in tension with what you need for yourself, so there's a dialogue within you about needs of self versus other. In why you choose relationships, karmically there are missteps. Probably in some other life you make a commitment because your parents think it makes a good match. Whether you're a boy or a girl, you can advance the family's position – Cancer/10th house South Node – by making a certain choice and then you spend 30 years with someone. You give this person children or you have children with this person and you don't love him or her. So there's a thing about needing to retool how you commit to things and what is seen to be really important.

The Persephone in the 7th kind of echoes it because it represents where we need to be abducted, and you needed to be abducted into situations that offer fairness and in which you can create harmony and balance and be happy within partnership. But that it is square to the nodes tells of an unresolved issue about where relationship takes you.

239

So now, a 20th/21st century adult woman can abduct herself in and out of relationships that do and don't work – that's the evolution of that, for you to make choices in this life that you probably didn't have an opportunity to make in other lives. I'm also reading intuitively that there's some life in which "they" are telling you – and you're like a 14-year old girl and are being promised to this guy down the street, in 3 years you'll marry – and you're very clear: "no!" You refuse to be abducted into what doesn't work and then the tension that that causes. Because this 10th-house Cancer South Node is about reputation. You're going to say something?

Anne: Yes. I'm in a new relationship for several months now, and I cautiously approaching it from a different place. I know what limits and boundaries are now – I certainly didn't know that before. It's pretty interesting!

Tom: That's karmic healing for you.

Anne: It feels that way.

Tom: To get to the place where something feels new.

Anne: And it feels healthy. Wherever the relationship goes, I'm not going to that old place. I'm just living it, letting it happen, and letting it unfold. Not trying to control it and so now, to me, it seems to have its own life and I know that it's a learning process for me.

Jillian: It's that Jupiter going through your 8th right now, just noticing that.

Tom: Those are the squares to the nodes. The only conjunction to the North Node is the IC, which is the beginning of the 4th house. It's a bit out of order because it

240

requires that we talk about step 4 for a moment, but let's do it. With the North Node conjunct the IC there's an extra emphasis to know inner needs and truth – what's really going on inside you. What you need, how you need to do it, what is the reality – Capricorn – about what makes people connected. It's kind of an evaluation of bloodline connections versus open-hearted friend connections in comparison with people you create family with in adulthood over time. And to weigh those things. One theme is getting very realistic about what is happening on the inside. So you're being confronted with that psychotherapist and wondering what you're supposed to say – that's from the 10th house. The 4th-house answer is, "I have to feel into what's really happening and then I eventually can tell you." But being in touch with that foundation.

When I talk about the parts of us getting shoved into the basement – kind of a different basement conversation – in the mansion of your psyche, there is this thing about the 4th house being our emotional foundation. Sometimes that is like the basement of a house, where our roots are. Getting conscious of who you are, what you need, and what is really happening is so important for you.

Step number 3 is the South Node ruler. South Node's Cancer so we look for the Moon and that's with Jupiter in Scorpio in the 2nd house. Within this context of a family that doesn't talk about emotions and people don't really know what they feel, you live in the house of trying to figure out self-worth and self-esteem (2nd). You live through the lens of digging to find the truth (Scorpio) but you're in a context where people don't know they feel but you need to figure out what you feel. They can't teach you that. There's that inherent tension between the South Node and the South Node ruler.

Moon is with Jupiter so you are going to have the capacity to develop a very buoyant optimism and self-esteem but you also have the capacity to get derailed from that because of intense emotions or pessimism. You know the power of optimism within you – it's almost like a superhero power if you can get to a positive place you can change your life around you but it's easy to get stuck in the opposite. So that's how you show up, as this South Node ruler, in the context in which people aren't really in touch with emotional stuff you are deeply in touch with stuff yet you don't have training or exposure to how it could or should be done.

That South Node ruler is squared by Saturn-Vesta in Pisces in the 5th and that brings the energy of friction from authority figures who take up a lot of space and who might not be clear about what's true or what is really going on. There could be a rule without foundation that then is pressed upon you. And you, South Node ruler, live in Scorpio and that means wanting an answer to "why is this rule in place?" and they can't answer you because they never got an answer when they were trained years ago. They might have given up with asking "why?" but you can't give up.

Candace: The pit bull.

Anne: I'm an archaeologist – I've been digging all my life!

Tom: Surrounded by people who don't know where the shovels are and don't understand what could possibly be under the surface.

Anne: Everybody else isn't asking all these questions all the time.

Tom: That's a thing with living Scorpio energy, and you also have Sun-Moon in Scorpio, which we'll get to. But when we live it karmically we are looking below the surface but we're surrounded by people who probably can't or don't want to. I think take this example from somebody else but there's a little kid at a dinner table, at a family gathering, who says something about the uncle who's an alcoholic: "Why is Uncle Jimmy always drunk?" And he's responded to with an admonishment that that's inappropriate, we don't talk about that. The realities of how things are really working – you keep bringing the question, "Can we just talk about this?" It's wanting to bring Pluto to the surface to be real.

Anne: Yeah.

Jillian: Pluto and Jupiter-Moon are trine each other and Pluto and Moon are in mutual reception.

Tom: Yeah, it underscores that need to have that kind of conversation out in the open.

Then we go to the 4th step of the process, the North Node. We talked about that some. There's a real need to know who you are and what you need but to do something about it. Coming from a Cancer South Node, I'm wondering if earlier in life you had any prejudices against being Capricorn, which is about structured, realistic, sacrifice in order to achieve greater goals, and long-term plans?

Anne: Could you ask that in a different way?

Tom: Sure. Sometimes within us there are prejudices about "those kinds of people" regarding our North Node symbolism. The South Node ruler for you, Moon, is squared by Saturn, the North Node ruler. So I talk about getting realistic about the inner quest, about seeing what it is that you actually need, what makes you tick, etc., but I'm wondering if you had to grow into being willing to do that even though nobody could show you how to do it. Did you have to become willing?

Anne: Oh, yes. I made a deep, deep commitment to myself at the time of that divorce. Consciously at that time I started this spiritual journey or path and I've done a lot of work over the last two years with a spiritual mentor and healer. So far I've healed from the sexual abuse. I love my father. All I choose to look at now are the wonderful things about him. I've forgiven my ex-husband finally – after a long time. I have a relationship with my younger son that had been very strained for many years. All because I started sending love and nothing but love. I've learned so much about being here and everything is energy. I'm so aware of what energy I'm projecting and what energy I'm feeling from other people. Sometimes it looks to be very difficult – some of the energy I feel from other people. Learning how to deal with that is a bit of a challenge right now and sometimes I'm in a situation where I feel way too much energy. I don't like going to Costco – I hate it! It's too big! [group laughs] I don't like being in large crowds of people. It's just too much energy. And so my own energy is what I'm really focused on right now, and how I'm with that energy in relationships. I find myself – I'm going to a book study group and we're studying a book called *Soul Evolution*, which is channeled by a group called the Serina. I don't know if you're familiar with that.

Tom: No.

Anne: It's the most wonderful book. A man appeared in our study group who was coming down from Ellensburg. He came in one day with a copy and wondered if we were interested in studying it as a group. I love to read and volunteered to take it home and preview it. And I started going through it and it was my kind of book. I took it back to the group and highly recommended it and it is wonderful – all about energy and the fact that we are all beings of energy. Now that man comes and goes – I'm sure that he came just to bring us that book – I know he did. There are things in there that I completely understand but that I can't always put them into words – there's just a knowingness I have. And I had some very powerful spiritual and psychic experiences when I was studying art, related to a class called Anthropology of Religion. Between that and my art classes I was going and painting before I saw a video for instance in that class. And the first time I stepped off the plane on the Greek Island of [inaudible] I knew I had been there before. I know I was a Native

American before. Sometimes this knowingness gets to be a bit too much! [laughs]

Tom: I know – I have that, too. [group laughs] I relate to that.

Anne: I can see it. So I find myself in this study group recently, and I don't know I'm going to say these things but I just open my mouth and start saying them. And recently I was reading this book … when I lived in Port Townsend I went to a week-long lecture series taught by a man from Antioch College in Seattle. He was a Jungian psychologist and he specialized in interpreting dreams. He had lived in Hiroshima for 10 years at least and he worked with survivors there and interpreted dreams for them and worked with them from a psychological standpoint. He told us about being in a hospital with some of the survivors and there was this medicine man from Africa who was there at the same time. When they left that hospital that medicine man said to this man, "I must take responsibility for this." And then he repeated it. And I know what he meant. I know that we are all responsible for everything – everything! Because we put that energy out there and it's time to look at what we're doing with our energy, isn't it?

Tom: It is.

Anne: And so start spouting things like this now in this study group and I think afterwards, "Oh my gosh! What did I say?" [group laughs] Just after we assassinated Osama Bin Laden and all these people on the TV were shown celebrating this and I thought, "no, no, no!! Where's our humanity?"

Tom: You said some things that bring in different parts of the chart like Venus-Neptune in the 12th – psychic art stuff – but for you to speak up about what's important to you all reflects a grounded foundation in that 4th house. "Realistically, what makes me tick? Who am I? What do I want to say?" I'm just pointing out that that reflects the North Node a lot though it brings in other parts of you.

Anne: I don't know what I'm going to say – it just comes out. It shocks me sometimes.

Tom: Great! With a 10th-house South Node we're trained to be respectful or, at least, appropriate, but if you have to say something you have to say it. And that's the 4th-house North Node: you have to bring out what's real. Because of the 10th-house South Node you have the possibility to get attention in public so as long as you speak from your heart, you'll feel fine. Thank you for all of that. I'm glad you came to this – I'm really glad you're here.

Candace: Me, too.

Jillian: So the South Node is what we're comfortable with, North Node is what we're not so comfortable with. When the North Node is conjunct the Nadir or the Descendant that's one thing, but with the Midheaven and Ascendant – they are how you appear to people. For instance she will look very Cancerian and Libran. When the North Node is conjunct one of those points and it's something uncomfortable for us to go to, how does that affect how other people see us or our comfort level embodying that sign?

Tom: That's really what that's about – the person's comfort level embodying that part of the self. The Midheaven, the beginning of the 10th house, is just a visible point – just who we appear to be. The North Node there would be about consciously experiencing what that's like and being comfortable with it. In that case what you have is an indicator that the family system could not train you how to live in the world.

Group: Wow.

Tom: Let's say that Anne's nodes were reversed and that Midheaven is on the Cancer North Node. It would mean that the family system is teaching her how to be Capricorn/4th house – inner. They would not be teaching her that if she wants to be a geologist then she has to go to college and get this certain kind of degree and training and a post-doc and all that – they can't teach her that. They can't tell her how to plan a long-term vision. But with this South Node where it is, what Anne's people *could* teach her is, if she said she wanted to have a particular profession, somebody in her family would probably be happy to advise her on practical ways to make that happen. I mean, there might or might not have been ideas about what women are supposed to do but the point is that they would understand more about things that work in the world because the South Node is in the 10th on the Midheaven. They didn't know how to talk about the emotional side of things. If it were reversed they might be all about emotions and not understand how to be in the world – they might have jobs they hate. They might have terrible relationships with bosses because they're not sure how to get what they want and need. It's about being in public but also dealing with the fact of people seeing you. So a North Node on a Midheaven would also be that you have to be comfortable being seen.

Jillian: What about the Ascendant?

Tom: Which one do you, North Node on the Ascendant?

Jillian: Yeah.

Tom: So you are seen as something. Let's say that it's a Libra Ascendant. People will make assumptions about that mask – people will see something about you. You can't help but show up as whatever the Ascendant is because you naturally carry the energy. But with the North Node there we bring in self-assertion – actively working the Ascendant – choosing to show up, making a decision about how you're going to act socially when you don't know people. It might be a default Libra expression without any choice or comfort about it. And think about healthy Ascendants and 1st houses. It can be a feeling like, "I'm just going to show up, interact with you, and look you in the eye." With the North Node there, they are not trained to do that. Their people defer to others – the 7th-house South Node. This house axis is about self-definition. 1st house: "I am." 7th house: "Well, I'm taking cues about how I am because I can see who you are and how I relate to you." Ach, laborious and complicated! So if you have a 7th-house South Node there could be a tendency in you to defer to others or to expect others to defer to you. The 1st-house

North Node or on the Ascendant done well would be just showing up – without apology, without hesitation or editing. You might see everybody else but you might not try to adapt to them, you might not try to be a chameleon. You might not have any inkling that people do that. You're just showing up.

Jillian: Thank you.

Tom: You're welcome.

Michael

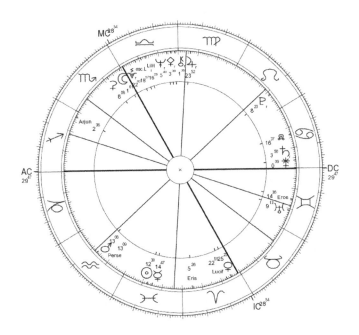

March 3, 1945, 4:35 AM, Deer Lodge, MT

Tom: Let's get into Michael's chart. We start with the 1st step, Pluto and the soul's intended empowerment journey. This is retrograde in Leo in the 7th house and it's close to the edge of the 8th but I'm going to read it in the 7th at least for now. The soul-level intention is to become empowered within relationships – 7th house – through one-on-one interactions and in a Leo way, which means to become empowered by showing up as who he really is. There may be some layering of debris about not doing that and then hoping other people see who you really are but they might not. This is about learning responsibility within relationship to tell others who you are.

Let's say you show up just as who you are but I've made assumptions about who you are, making it impossible to really connect with you. I'm looking you in the eye and listening to the words that you are using but we are not energetically on the same page. That's going to be hard for you because you need to recognize the individuality of others within your relationships but you need to receive that, too. What we don't always get about the Venus/Libra/7th house archetype is that we are responsible for showing who we are. We're hoping the other person sees us but we're responsible for showing up. So there's a cue for you, Michael.

Michael: Thank you.

Tom: You're welcome. There's an element here of joy in relationships, because we're talking about joy, fun – needing relationships to have a certain simplicity so that they're enjoyable. Everything doesn't have to be complex all the time. But he's also wired at the soul level to learn about what it takes to make relationships work so things do get complicated sometimes. This retrograde of Pluto is about inventing his own relationship wheel. Everybody around him has ideas on how to do this relationship and that relationship – what it takes, what it means – but he's got to become empowered via his own means, his own way of doing it. What a Pluto in the 7th that's retrograde can experience – and you can tell us yes or no if this resonates

– the having of relationships earlier in life that end up being intense proving grounds, whether marriages or not. You're learning intensely about relationship dynamics but you have to have some kind of stable, committed structure in which to do it. So your first serious relationship might have been an incredible amount of work until you learned about who you are within relationship. But then other relationships later, when you make certain decisions, can get easier because you're doing it differently. But you have to have an incubator first.

Michael: One that challenged my trust and my decision in another person if I was going to sink my heart into it, and then suddenly had new things come up and I wondered if I should be guarded for that part. And then I had to develop connections at that point.

Tom: I said proving grounds but we could also say test or laboratory. And at the time, you're in it but now you can see it was kind of a practice run. In the context of the soul's journey you need these incubators to figure out how you are going to choose to behave in relationship – that's what the whole point is. Two threads: A) "How I'm going to show up?" and B) "How I'm going to receive the other?" "How am I going to learn about what I need, how to talk about that, and also honor what the other person needs?" Because individuality within relationship – Leo in the 7th house – is the name of the game.

7th-house stuff becomes a unit – people going together – and head off in one direction. Perhaps off into the sunset or off holding hands and skipping together, but there is this directionality together, while the Leo thing points to the importance of your individuality to be intact for your happiness and health within relationships.

Michael: Alongside the other?

Tom: Yes, two individuals choosing to skip down the sidewalk together instead of losing individuality.

With this Pluto retrograde, how his parents, grandparents, cousins, and siblings did it doesn't matter. He's got to forge his own way through this relationship stuff. Even if he gets tons of great advice it won't work for him.

There is a square to Moon-Ceres – another Moon in Scorpio square Pluto. And also the opposition to Mars-Persephone in Aquarius. Let's start with the opposition. Mars-Persephone in Aquarius are in the 2nd house. When somebody's Pluto is opposed by a body in the 2nd – and we talked about this with Glenna's Pisces Sun opposing Virgo Pluto – you are opposed by somebody who is not movable, who is standing his or her ground. Mars indicates that there is an aggressive energy to this. Aquarius can indicate difference and uniqueness but also can be harsh. There's an element here of criticism or being blocked that he has received in his relationships, probably he's had intimate, long-term relationship with somebody who really challenges him but there's a lot of love. But it can also be from outside, having difficult energy opposing your relationships. Does that make sense to you, Michael?

Michael: Yeah.

Tom: With Persephone there –

Michael: What was her theme?

Tom: Abduction.

Michael: Is that a forced position?

Tom: It can be. Somebody else bringing you assertive energy that changes everything.

Michael: It could be good.

Tom: It could be great.

Michael: For me it could be real good.

Tom: This is the phrase that comes to me: as you seek the best way to get on the same page with somebody you're involved with – even a friend – something that can change everything is this very forceful change that confronts what you perceive you need. So someone brings an energy to you that is like an unshakeable, unmovable object and you're trying to get on the same page. But that person's lack of willingness to adapt teaches you about you.

That person will not get on the same page with you. It can look like struggle and conflict even if there's love and then it shows you your need. You'll manifest these people because you need to learn about Mars and Persephone through opposition. That aspect could depict two gun fighters ready to shoot each other down if they feel threatened and it could also be that I'm looking straight at you and you're looking straight at me – I can see you in a way that you cannot see yourself, and you see me in a way that I cannot see myself. So am I willing to learn from you or do I feel threatened?

Michael: There's that love element – I'd be more willing to stay in that relationship when there's love. That's attractive to me: "How did you get so smart?"

Tom: That's right. Because we were talking about Mars square Pluto with these ladies, the opposition says that it is also possible that violence can come to you. Perhaps you haven't experienced that but it is possible.

Michael: Like violence coming to me from that person opposing me?

Tom: Like people coming at you, threatening you, picking on you.

Glenna: People that make you feel overpowered.

Michael: I know people in my life who are like that but I haven't experienced that.

Tom: It's not his karma – perfect! I wanted to point it out in case there was a juicy story that could use some understanding.

Annette: But you did – weren't you a teacher at the college for … ?

Michael; For fencing. [group laughs]

Tom: That's you doing the energy. Maybe he doesn't have karma of being overpowered by Mars and that's awesome – we're all happy to hear that. I just wanted to bring it up just in case.

Michael: But it's useful to think about that.

Tom: It basically says that Mars stuff – aggression, assertion, martial arts, war, violence, rescue, defense – stands opposite you in all these lives and different experiences give you the opportunity to learn about taking action even though you're confronted. "I don't know if I would do it that way but that's very successful, so let me figure out how to do that."

Michael: I see the opposition sometimes when I feel I don't have the confidence to go do something. And then someone tells me I've already done it – "we *know* you can do it" – and tells me to activate that Mars, to get in there and give it a try. But some part of me will say, "I don't think I can do that."

Tom: That's it.

Michael: And then Mars says, "Yes, I can do that."

Tom: And needing to own the Mars.

Glenna: What about this abduction idea? If Mars is with your will and Persephone is right there with it?

Tom: He needs to be abducted into asserting his will, which is a way of standing up for the self and having boundaries.

Michael: It's happened that I've called for help and people tell me I've already done that. [group laughs]

Tom: They're reflecting to you things you're not quite sure are true but probably are. That's part of the Mars opposing Pluto – other people are Mars. Other people have the boldness.

Michael: Yes.

Tom: Other people save kittens from trees.

Michael: Yeah.

Tom: Other people put out fires, you know, and climb ladders and help people. Good for you to own this part of you and then we're going to talk about your South Node, which is in the house of Mars – the 1st house. I think that will bring up more layers and will be revelatory and instructive.

He needs to be abducted into original ways of doing Mars and that will help his self-esteem because it's in the 2nd house. But he might not think that Mars is his because it opposes Pluto, the soul's mission. In some lives you've been blocked by Mars people. That you are not overtly carrying the karma and trauma of war is great, I love to see it, but you've at times been blocked by Mars. You might not have developed meaning about it – the beliefs that provide meaning to painful experiences – when somebody blocks you.

Michael: I think it affects my confidence in many ways, thinking I can't do something.

Tom: Right – others see you as capable, clear, and in the moment.

Michael: Others ask me what's the problem, and I don't know. I just don't think I can do it. It could be this tension.

Tom: That's right. In some lives you could have been told by martial people, "You can't do this." A thread of this could be a kid who doesn't get picked for the sports team enough, for some reason. Like maybe they perceive you're not tall enough to play basketball.

Michael: All of my sports experiences in school I never got picked because I wasn't quite big enough.

Tom: I'm feeling into it – and that's not even just from this life but is a repeat. This feeling from other lives is of not being like everyone else because they don't want you to play with them. The first thing I got a moment ago that I put on a shelf for a moment: "I want to join the army." And then looking at you and saying, "You're too nice of a guy. You're kind of a sweet guy – I don't think you can cut it." And you saying, "I want to fight for my country" with the response, "I don't think you got what it takes, kid – call me in 2 years." But you're so deflated that you never call back. Like you show up when you're 16 is what I'm getting at and they're like, "oh, we can't take you quite yet." But that kind of challenge to your mettle.

But over time, if you believe that they might be right, then you'll start to believe that maybe you can't do this or that because Mars people oppose you. So you haven't experienced it as trauma but as something else. It's nice to see because a lot of people with kind of signature might.

Michael: It's a reminder that those are indicators that I know I've experienced – told I "might be too short for the basketball team and too little for the football team, so you'd better go do something else."

Tom: That's a karmic thing.

Candace: I'm just getting this energy, the fact that it's Aquarian. Let's bring in the Aquarian "I'm so different." You're a little bit different male, not the typical Mars alpha male. "So I feel a little bit alien" – abduction. Being a male with an alienation, with that sense of "I am the fencing instructor." When you grow up to be the fencing instructor you're like, "I'm going to show you this and you're going to think it's just the coolest thing in the world" and when you're doing it you feel empowered, in your center. It takes you a different way to do Mars.

Tom: If all he wanted when he was a kid to be a football player and they wouldn't let him do it, then fencing would look like a cheap substitute that never would be fulfilling. But you're doing it and that's great but from that vantage point it might have looked like it's not fulfilling – from the outside. [group "ohhhs!"}

Michael: It wasn't as strong of a thing to be doing.

Tom: Exactly. So this is a karmic thing for you. This is in the 2nd house: how can you develop self-esteem by owning the Mars you *do* have?

Group: Yeah! Right!

Candace: In its individualistic, unique, original way.

Michael: That is so clear!

Tom: Your Mars comes out through the energy work that's physical, yoga, even the music but it's different than the alpha male kind of model.

Glenna: And I would say ahead of its time.

Candace: Way ahead of its time! [group claps]

Tom: Yes! Just because you didn't get picked for the team doesn't mean that you're not masculine in a wonderful way. It just means that in that particular social context you don't fit what they think it would look like.

Michael: But I have females who help me, who say, "The male in you is fine."

Glenna: It's a maverick, actually.

Tom: This is a lot about this story because – and I'm going to jump around here, forgetting the 4-step method for a minute – the South Node in the 1st house in Capricorn says that you're conditioned – there is nothing more masculine. So you're coming from family systems where there's an understanding of what a man is supposed to be like.

Michael: Totally. A family of 5 brothers.

Tom: Where are you in the birth order?

Michael: First.

Tom: You're the first?

Michael: I'm the smallest so my father said, "You're so little, you'd better learn boxing or something because you're gonna need it."

Tom: And did you?

Michael: I did.

Tom: Oh, I love this! Was there a military thing in your family at all? Your dad or grandfather, or your brothers?

Michael: A real devotion to it. All of them.

Tom: A 1st-house South Node can indicate conditioning through war or even just involvement with the military, the kind of idea of masculinity we've been running in our culture for quite a while – the hypermasculine way of doing military.

Glenna: And here we have the abducted warrior.

Tom: Who has to be abducted into sports to prove that he's got mettle, that he's got substance. But the South Node ruler Saturn – where is it? It's retrograde in Cancer in the 7th house.

Group: Ohh!

Tom: That's what I wanted to get to out of order. In the 1st-house Capricorn thing – devotion to the military in the family history – you are Cancerian and in the 7th, the opposite house. You are trying to be soft and listen, trying to be a good listener, and you're trying to honor other people's needs. This would be a juicy story no matter where you were in the birth order but the soul's contracts with all these family members are specific – you're the first of 5 males in a Capricorn/1st house family.

Group: Leading the way with softness.

Tom: Yeah, even if they don't get it

Michael: No, not at all.

Tom: Are they all surviving?

Michael: Yeah, and they're all [makes muscle flexing gesture] – every one of them.

Tom: Versions of strength. This is a family that is shaped deeply by patriarchal philosophy and so he at the soul level has agreed to be a teacher for them for being an anti-patriarchal male. He has a Mars – he uses it. He's used it his entire life but it's not what they might expect. If you ask them they'll say you're not quite Mars enough.

If he came to me for a reading I would ask myself and then observe him to find the answer, "Does he have a problem being masculine?" I would see that no, he just does it in a Cancerian way. I would see that South Node ruler in the 7th –

Michael: The female in me has always been so strong and I'm not attracted to boys or something like that, but I feel I have a very different kind of take on being.

Tom: Your soul is saying, "Even if nobody gets it and I don't really understand what's happening, I'm going to hold space for people in this family system to have a model of masculinity that isn't only about guts and proving the self." A lot of men who are shorter in stature or smaller in size feel like they have to compensate. You were told you needed to learn boxing if you wanted to measure up. There'd be a lot of guys your size who would go to something like that to prove themselves because to live in this culture as a man who doesn't seem manly according to social expectations is hard. It's a whole family story about patriarchy.

Michael: Also, I was never attracted to that so I didn't feel like I had to get on the team. After a while I realized I didn't want to do that anyway. Kind of a weird reaction to that. My dad told me, "Buck up, buddy. Your 4 brothers are passing you up." But I was smart, and he liked that.

Tom: So he did value something about you.

Michael: He asked me to help run the store. He had my brothers stack things and do all that but he had me help run it. I got those kind of jobs.

Tom: So you were appreciated, just not for what they might have dreamed about when it came to boys?

Michael: Yes.

Annette: You mentioned you were told your brothers were always passing you up -- was there a constant pressure on you to – how did you go about holding that? Because it feels like you held it.

Michael: See, I had a lot of support from my grandmother that kind of insulated me, completely insulated me to keep me on my own path.

Tom: And she was masculine and feminine – she had both.

Michael: That was still a matriarchal French family, believe me. The matriarch was there making the money, bringing things in. And I learned from her. If she said I was doing well then after a while it didn't matter what anyone else said, and that was my star. It helped keep me going – confident in my choices.

Glenna: Where do you see the masculine and feminine grandmother?

Tom: Any teacher who really supports him has to have both in the same balance that he has, even if a different gender. To be able to recognize that in him.

Michael: That's why I've never noticed that a female was less than a male. So I've never had an issue about being more than females – in partnerships, with children, with anything.

Tom: Your Saturn in the 7th is also conjunct Juno so there is an emphasis for you on actually seeing who the other is. It might look in this cultural context like it's noble that he has this egalitarian outlook but the fact is he's made a point of really seeing who the other is.

Glenna: He's been working on it.

Tom: Many, many lives. It's important for him to show up to be fair and so he's looking ... I mean in any relationship, he sees the other. He doesn't see a woman in terms of patriarchal conditioning – he sees a woman as a human. He sees a man as a human, not as better than or "less than." He even see top dog and underdog as other people – he doesn't see them as underdog and top dog. He keeps showing up as committed (Juno) to being sensitive (Cancer) to the reality of the other (7th house). It will come out in particular relationships, too, but just on the level of basic interacting – honoring how somebody else is wired.

Annette: Is that like beyond you – like your soul has that going on before you get here?

Tom: I would offer that all of our souls know that but the eruption into space-time where we start to have separate identities and forget that we're Divinity – that's where we develop attitudes such as *you're "less than" and you're "more than"*. I don't want to put it on soul but I want to say that he's just made it his business over many lives to actually see what's in front of him. Juno's there so he's committed to this, and when you live in the 7th house through a Cancerian lens, you will see what's actually there in another person. Michael sees the look in the eyes of his mother if his father treats her as "less than." So he *sees* the other. He doesn't see hairstyle, curves, and dress – she's a woman and then the cultural assignation of value – he doesn't do that. He sees her as a person. He sees what's in front of him. He doesn't put a mask over what he sees. Even if they didn't get it on the personality level, from the soul level that's a gift for the rest of his family. They are learning through having him as a family member.

I'm glad to hear that your father did appreciate you. In some other life contexts maybe that wouldn't happen but they'd still be learning at the soul level from you.

Michael: I'm more appreciated now by my brothers.

Tom: Right.

So we're still in step 2 though I jumped ahead a bit. Square the South Node are Venus-Lucifer in Aries in the 3rd house and Lilith-Vesta in Libra in the 9th house. This talks about the family system and family karma – what they could and couldn't teach him. Venus has to do with value system as well as relationships. There are reasons that relationships are chosen – and this echoes Anne's Juno in the 7th square the nodes – that are an issue. You could sit down and analyze why you perceive your parents got married, why they wanted to be together, and you can see some glistening threads of things that you can learn about your own relationships that would benefit you. It also means that in various lives you have picked relationships for reasons that don't really serve you. Earlier I was talking about the first serious relationship you would have had would serve as an incubator for you to learn about what you need in relationship because of the Pluto in the 7th house and this fits with that. Pluto in the 7th and Venus square the nodes is an emphasis: "I really need to learn about this relationship stuff. I really need to figure this out and make some choices that feel like tripping over my shoe laces and then learning from them." The Lucifer part of it is about picking relationships in which you get to shine and be equally represented. In this life you might go back and forth but you have in some lives an extreme of picking a relationship where you get to be the center of attention and in other lives you defer to the other person; you won't shine. And your values aren't ever honored because you don't really show up and tell the other person what you want and like. You're exploring what all that is.

Michael: Those are two extremes.

Tom: Yes, vacillating back and forth. Sometimes finding more of a middle ground but not always – and the ideal of course is to find it. The emotional archaeology part of it is to look at examples from your life that might fit those two extremes, did you assign meaning to why you made a choice or why something happened the way it did? The meaning could be changed. The real meaning is that you're learning something – you didn't make a mistake. The reason, for example, it happened is not that you did something wrong if that's applicable, or that the other person did – the reason is you're learning. You don't know it all already. You're trying to figure out where on this continuum "reasonable" is, where "good give and take" is.

The Lilith-Vesta in Libra in the 9th square the nodes: Vesta has to do with something we take really seriously. Lilith in Libra is going to have a lot to do with equality within relationship. The Lilith story, which is represented by 4 chapters in the *Living Myth* book, in part has to do with figuring out how to have equality within relationship given this patriarchal training that most people have: men are supposed to be like this, women are supposed to be like that. There's not a lot of wiggle room and if there is, something's wrong. We live in 2011 and we don't think that way but we've been trained for 6,000 years to think that way. This conjunction says that it's really, really important for you to figure out the equality thing, what's fair, but also how to create it. Not just to note what's unfair and address with people what they've done to you but to see your part in all of it and how you are creating it; how you are creating your reality within relationship.

So we've got 4 things here about relationship: 1) Venus square the nodes, 2) Lilith-Vesta square the nodes in Libra – a Venus sign, 3) Pluto in the 7th house – a house of Venus, and 4) North Node in the 7th house – "I need to learn about give and take." There couldn't be more indications of needing to learn about healthy relating. If you approach it with that Cancerian/7th house idea of, "But I'm listening to you and sensitive to your needs" then that's great, *and* make sure you show up. Make sure you're taking responsibility for telling the other person what you need, too. It can be easy for someone in that position to default to what others need and you need to make sure you show up.

Michael: To be an equal in the relationship. It's very attractive to me if the female has that strong energy, and then I really don't have to do anything. [group laughs]

Tom: That's right!

Michael: Not that I'm lazy, it's just a strong force and I really love that strong force. It helps me be stronger but I don't have to be equal.

Tom: But make sure you're there.

Michael: Yeah, I gotta make sure I show up.

268

Jillian: You bring a different style of strength.

Michael: And I've met that with two female best friends because they were so strong but I had something to offer that was strong, too, and I hadn't seen that as a strength. But it is.

Tom: We kind of talked already about the symbolism of Michael's North Node because the South Node ruler is already there. Because he already gets it energetically and emotionally, what we want to do with the North Node is contrast the habit patterns of the South Node and how to leave them behind if they don't work. Because the South Node ruler is here you already have the skill set but whenever there is tension within you about being that way, we want to relieve the tension. Resolving some of the tension from the past will help you be in the North Node. This is all about coming from people who don't understand you.

With this North Node let's talk about the karma, or beliefs that might be in place, about why other people feel the way that you are naturally wired isn't okay. What I'm going to say kind of skips a couple of steps but I want to show you the finish line with this: Absolute, utter compassion and forgiveness for how they did and didn't treat you, could and couldn't understand you. Because how parts of you might have interpreted their treatment of you – talking about family and those people who didn't pick you for the teams. Anybody who didn't get your version of masculinity. How they treated you had to do with their conditioning and isn't about you. How those people treated you is about their own perceived limitations and lack of imagination.

Michael: I've had Candace refer to this when asking me, "Well, what voice is that?" When I tell her how I think something is and she asks who said that – it doesn't sound like me. I learned to turn those voices down and I'm really learning about them and how to identify them.

Tom: That's a level of karmic healing for you to just let everyone else's voices go. But of course it's natural for any of us to take on the voices of the others because we're trying to do the right thing and they seem like they know what they're doing. "They see me, so what they're thinking must be true." You already have the willingness to listen to the other and be engaged in relationship in a Cancerian, heart-centered way. It seems to me that the next step would be making sure that you give back all those voices and get that they were trying to train you, understanding that anything you took on was to try to fit in while trying to do the right thing.

The other thing about living in the 7th house – it's not just about saying "yes" to others but also saying "no thanks" to them. It's easy when we talk about a business negotiation or you're selling a house and I make a bid – well, you make a counteroffer and then we go back and forth – we discuss it and we make decisions. But in personal relationships we're not used to saying, "That doesn't work for me. No thanks. I have to do another thing." You have become conditioned to say "yes, please" when it works and also "no thanks" when it doesn't work –

that rounds out your Cancer/7ᵗʰ house experience. Understand that when you say "no thanks" to someone you're not saying, "I don't love you." You're saying, "That just isn't what I can do." If I reject your idea I'm not rejecting you but sometimes we can think or feel it might be, or must be.

For you to also be willing to say "no" – from a heart-felt place is important.

Michael: And hopefully it's understood the other way. "There's a boundary here – I have to tell you." Setting the boundary and giving the feedback in the moment. It's open – come on in. Let's set something up.

Tom: It rounds out the karmic education for your North Node, the thing that you haven't really gotten fully. You've gotten part of it because the South Node ruler is in Cancer – so you've done some of it – but to round out the education by adding that to it. And that's hard for anyone living a Venus story and as I said, he has 4 Venus things – each karmic thing is a Venus thing. Learning how to say "no" is big. And it doesn't have to end in arguments, fights, rejection, being cut off, or having to leave. People living Venus stories – especially with Pluto in the 7ᵗʰ – will need to learn at some point about healthy conflict as well. [group laughs]

Michael: Hmm, healthy conflict – that's a nice combination.

Tom: I didn't mention it when I talked about Pluto in Libra but it's relevant for all the people in that generation as well as those with Pluto in the 7ᵗʰ or Pluto conjunct

271

Venus. They need to learn how to fight but that it doesn't have to be terrible, violent, or angry. *But I do need to learn to stand up to you and respect when you need to stand up to me.* Conflict doesn't have to lead to terrible things.

Michael: Healthy conflict.

Tom: But with compassion, understanding, and "I love you and there's a problem we need to work out." Not "I love you but…" – "I love you *and…*" When you come from this Venus place that your soul has been exploring through your human lives, you have certain ideas about what arguing would look like. Or conflict. What would happen. That's an expectation in place because you haven't really experienced it. You don't really know what it looks like. Each of us has to learn at some point –

Michael: Rather than ignore it and pretend it's not even there – I know how to do that. I have to say it is here.

Tom: *And that I want to talk about it with you. I'm going to feel what I'm feeling and think about it and I want you and I to discuss it openly.* Okay, good – you got that.

That's what I see with your North Node and learning what it really takes to create relationship. It isn't giving in, being nice, and opening to what the other is experiencing. It's equality – showing up and being responsible for being one member of a pair.

Michael: Thank you, Tom.

Tom: You're welcome.

Summer

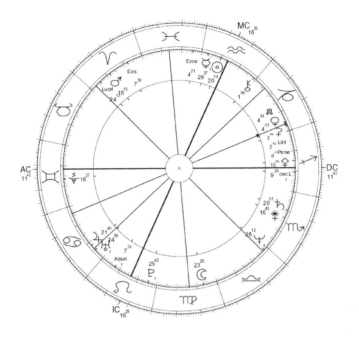

February 9, 1955, 12:14 PM, Des Moines, IA

Tom: Our first step is to look at Pluto. Leo in the 4th house and retrograde. This is a soul-level intention to learn about empowerment through dealing with emotions but also being connected to people. In the 4th house it represents this inner emotional world or reality and is an echo of the Pluto in Cancer we talked about with Anne. But in the 4th house it is also directly related to family history and who we in our family are because of the trajectory of history – genealogy, energetic and literal inheritances, and things, attitudes, and behaviors that come down through time or are passed down through families. This is about being defined in many lives by family and by belonging and connectedness.

Summer: That's what I came from, right?

Tom: That's what you've been experiencing a lot of because your soul intends that you become empowered through it. In some lives you are disconnected and that teaches soul about family. For example, leaving home young and never coming back whether positive or negative circumstances. In some lives you might be adopted. In other lives like this one you're a twin in a family with – how many kids?

Summer: Six.

Tom: All these different ways of learning about togetherness and connectedness. In Leo it's important to find joy in that connectedness but also it's important for you to be recognized as an individual, which is part of the thing with being a twin. She has an identical twin sister if anyone didn't know that yet. The soul says, "I need to become empowered by being recognized as an individual within my family." And in some lives you'd be the only kid and were lonely because of it and in other lives you're one of 6 – there are different ways of learning about that.

One of the things that can happen with this setup is the need to learn how to feel special within the family group. Because this is a marker of acknowledging that we're all equals in this group but you also need to feel special within that group so there can be some tension in there for you. You see?

Summer: Yeah. I had to kind of find my way to be able feel individual somehow.

Tom: Right. Where are you and your sister in the birth order?

Summer: Spring is 3 minutes older than me.

Tom: I mean where are you two in the order of births in the family?

Candace: Numbers 4 and 5 out of 6.

Tom: And how many years separate the oldest and youngest kids?

Summer: 10 years.

Tom: Thank you.

Your Pluto is retrograde so you have to find your own way of being special – this whole idea of inventing your own wheel thing. Being an identical twin is kind of a classical, stereotypical setup for this: "How can I feel special? I'm just like her. Or maybe we're not the same, but we are, but we're unique, but we're totally the same – but we're not." [group laughs] You know? This question about how you are special. Especially being real young. Did your parents dress you alike? Because that's very common.

Summer: Oh, yes.

Tom: Aspects to Pluto include a square to Saturn in Scorpio in the 6th. The soul's empowerment mission is about this connectedness, togetherness, and learning how to feel special while learning how to belong. A square to Saturn says that the soul intends to learn about respect, authority, maturity, and morality by being pressured by it through people and situations that bring those energies. Every single time that you have had an issue with an authority figure or one has had an issue with you – either way – pushing you out of your power – it's actually to teach you different ways that it can happen so that you can make better choices to embody it yourself.

The Saturn is in Scorpio so these people drawn to you need to be intense and they need to work to push your buttons of if you deserve to feel special.

Summer: Say that again.

Tom: They will be the kind of people who will work hard to push the button of "oh, so you think you're special?" These are the kind of people who would rather have you conform.

Summer: Meaning me? I would rather see me conform?

Tom: You're going to draw people to try to pressure you to conform. But you are clear you need to explore what it means to feel special. These people tell you to fall in line.

Summer: Exactly! I stepped right into the Christian church – gave my hippie clothes away and was like, "I will be a doormat." [group laughs] But it gave me a sense of tribe and spirituality, too, to a certain extent.

Tom: In some lives, however, this conflict arises: you either have a sense of tribe *or* you get to do what you want. A baseline tension in a bunch of your lives including this one is try to figure out how to be special and not give in. How to be empowered and belong. "Do I have to take on your beliefs in order for you to love me?" In some places, times, and families, yeah, you actually kind of do and that's what you've been learning about. And then other times you don't but are conditioned to think you might – and it gets a little messy because then you're waiting for something to happen that may or may not happen.

Emotional archaeology on this one: when you have felt pressured to have to give something up in order to belong, what did it mean about you, them, life, and God? That's the process of digging through this aspect. You probably liked your hippie clothes – that version of you. That identity. Obviously internal identity you carry with you everywhere but they were probably important as an external symbol – they fit with who you were.

Summer: Who I was at the time.

Tom: And you gave them up to do this other thing so you could have tribe. This tension in different lives is about the question if you can have tribe and be who you know you are.

Summer: And seriously, that is what life has taught me. It's taught me that I don't have to make choices to conform or to please other people. To listen to my own heart and stand for what I believe.

Tom: That's karmic healing – that's great. That's the best that I could offer you about this aspect in this conversation.

Annette: I know a little bit of your history, and I think it's interesting that you went off and tried to start your own tribe, your own community – in Hawaii.

Summer: I believe in community and am still into that. That particular situation was there to teach me. That community didn't really get going but I can see how it's taught me much.

Annette: When I'm with you I feel community – period.

Tom: Oh, yeah.

Group: Yeah!

Summer: I feel like I have a community in my heart because I think of myself and then all of us as one.

Tom: Good, because I think in some lives you don't ever get to that place because it's so hard to feel that you belong. It might go without saying but the ultimate state of evolution is for you to get that on the inside, carry the community in your heart. So that is great.

There's an echo of the square from Saturn to Pluto in the opposition from Sun and Mercury in Saturn's house, the 10th. This is about needing to learn about boldness and communication by feeling blocked by it, or up against a wall, or a deer caught in the headlights. That's another thing about the authority-figure echo here. You need to learn how to integrate these energies you've been blocked by. On the personality level – we keep talking about this – is just the inner CEO who's running the meeting in your psyche but karmically when you're opposed by the Sun it means that somebody who is very powerful and strong is trying to keep you from getting where you're trying to go. This is here about the soul-level mission of connection and community. I would bet that the situation that Annette just commented on that didn't take off had to do with somebody who was really, really powerful holding things up. Because you need a teacher like that to show you how to be powerful and then you can say, "Well, I want to be ¾ like that but not with the garbage."

Summer: Right.

Tom: To teach you – to show you how to do bold.

Summer: I can see that.

Tom: And then opposing Mercury, there's a need to learn to get clear in your head to have perspective on what you're really trying to get done and why. So these other people might be drawn because they communicate in a way that you need to adopt even if their motivation is different than yours. Not necessarily silver tongues or smooth talkers or liars but they have certain skills in the way they communicate that you need to learn to integrate for your own benefit. But you might feel like a deer in the headlights when you're with them.

Summer: Kinda, yeah! I just had this situation about two months ago. I told Candace and she looked at my chart and told me it's exactly what the chart says. This guy was coming in kind of pressing against the value of my silk, wanting it reduced. But he ended up teaching me about how to have compassionate language. I humbled myself and told myself I'm here to expand and to grow.

Tom: That's what we mean when we talk about taking the reflections, so that's good.

Summer: It wasn't easy.

Tom: No! Of course not. That anonymous guy at the festival was a karmic teacher for you.

Summer: So he was teaching me to communicate.

Candace: In your own way.

Tom: In your own way. For example you could think of how someone else might respond in that situation and could, in fact, think of many and analyze all of them. But you have to do it in your own way. That's part of the deer-in-the-headlights things because you have to respond creatively when you haven't been on this road before, you haven't done it before. In general, Mercury retrograde personality-wise – forget the karmic angle – means that the perception and communication function works differently. It means that learning works differently as does mental processing. Sometimes it can be literal reading and writing – the physical side of it – but that part of the self works differently.

Natally her communication will work differently and she has to forge her own road to the right way to learn and communicate. For example, when she's 8 years old in school and everyone learns something pretty much at the same pace but she's either 3 weeks ahead or 2 days behind.

Summer: More like two grades behind.

Tom: It might look like there's something wrong with you but your mind works differently – that's all it is. As it is we're just trying to get everybody moved through the cattle chute of the education system as easy as possible. So there's nothing wrong but it looks like that from their perspective. You grow up and realize there's nothing wrong but at the time it's just different.

Karmically, having retrograde Mercury opposing your Pluto means that other people's communication is weird and it blocks you. In other words, their communication styles aren't working normally and maybe you're trying to get something done but you can't get clear with them because their minds aren't clear. So now you are going to draw those people to you. It's to keep you on your toes so that you let your mind evolve. You let your self-awareness of how your mind works evolve. In the context of this guy at the festival being a karmic teacher for you, he puts you on the spot and you have to use your mind in a way that you've never used it. That's an opportunity for karmic healing because you get to use your mind in a conscious, proactive way.

As you've matured and become an adult you've observed that everyone's mind is unique but you had to grow into that awareness because when you were young it might have looked like something was wrong with you. People get worried about kids who don't learn at the "right" speed or if their handwriting doesn't get beautiful by the time they're 11 or something like that. Or if they don't spell things the way we're expected to spell. By the way, something I find fascinating: spelling in the English language was not standardized until Webster introduced some teaching materials in the early 19th century. Somehow he became the authority on how words should be spelled. If you go back to the 18th century and prior you find words spelled in ways that are crazy and then "sic" in brackets, like, "oh, that was wrong in the original." But it wasn't wrong. This Mercury retrograde thing in our times is interesting to me because we're supposed to be one version of normal. Prior to Webster in the early 1800s there was no standardization of spelling. Suddenly everyone had a standard to measure up to but before that, who cares how things are spelled? "Fairy" – how many different ways do we have to spell that?

Michael: At least 3.

Tom: That's what I'm thinking. And fay and fey and gay and gey. And if we read for example Shakespeare and it's not updated/edited, we find that. He's (or they're) consistent within his time and style but relative to other writers they have their own signatures. Including names! Anyway.

Michael: That was very helpful.

Tom: Good. Now those are the big, shiny aspects to Pluto, which is step 1. I want to move on to step 2, the South Node. This is in Cancer in the 2nd house just over the edge of the 2nd. We had an 8th house South Node with Jillian and we had two Plutos in the 8th with Jillian and Glenna. We've spent a lot of time on the 8th house and mentioning the 2nd house as somewhere to go. You're coming from the 2nd house and we want you to go to the 8th house so I'm going to talk about it a little differently. The South Node in the 2nd says that there's an emphasis in this karmic journey on self-sufficiency and whether or not you are self-sufficient is secondary. [group laughs] It's a focus on what the individual should be doing for him- or herself and how that translates into self-esteem including what skills do you possess that you can use to earn money to survive. So that you're in business for yourself doesn't surprise me because you have a karmic history of needing to rely on yourself or, at least, figure out how to work money in the right way. That's the South Node in the 2nd house.

In Cancer, it's viewed through the lens of emotion and attachment. It could be that you experience a lot of emotion about self-worth. There's something in the 2nd house to be said about the boot straps – pulling the self up by them – that you've had to do that in various lives including this one – that's a part of your karmic history.

Next is Eris square the nodes in the 11th. Again, Eris moves slowly and we all have it in Aries. I talked about it being related to strife and discord. When I used it in somebody's karmic story here I talked about chaos. The 11th house is about groups and society and is where social networks belong but also mobs of people. When it's positive you network and when it's negative you're a face in a crowd. Eris square the nodes from this house tells us that there's an element of social chaos that really affects the family system you come from. It could be that they are trying to have an orderly home but are living in a place that's full of all kinds of stuff that's going on. For example, in modern times your family lives in a house and you might be surrounded by 4 different skin colors and 5 different religions, and 6 languages all on your block. That would fit with trying to do one thing but having all these other influences – it can seem a little energetically chaotic. That's kind of a mild, benign example but one of stuff happening in our community around us that is a little scattered or something. I'm not getting the sense that it has a lot to say to us right now but I wanted to mention it for the record. But any square to the nodes means that we need to learn something new because we have certain assumptions and experiences that lead to habits. For you, what kind of group interests you is going to have an element of chaos to it, which we could look at as a positive thing about dynamism. That would be a positive way of looking at Eris re chaos, strife, and discord: things actually get to change, things can look ahead and be forward-looking. So you'd be drawn to hippie culture – you know what I mean?

Summer: Right.

Tom: Lots of signatures could lead to that.

Jillian: As far as the house placement and how it relates to long-term planning, Eris could also throw a monkey wrench into things, confusing long-term goals.

Tom: Thank you.

Summer: It really hasn't been easy to figure out what it is I want to do in life. It hasn't been clear. I've had to really dig. Early in life I also wasn't in touch with my feelings or my own inner world.

Tom: I see. Then the other aspect to the nodes is Venus-Ceres conjunct the North Node in Capricorn right on the cusp of the 8th house. To repeat, anything conjunct the North Node says that it wasn't available to us, we didn't get to experience it, in many lives. Venus on the North Node can say several things: "My value system didn't matter. I don't get to choose things. I don't get to choose relationships. I don't get to enjoy life." Ceres there says, "I didn't learn to nurture or take care of myself." These are in Capricorn so it's about realism and maturity, which is a slow process. Decisions can get made for 2nd-house reasons – which are often very practical and involve necessity and survival – but happiness, joy, and pleasure might get left out because of necessity. Tying in Jillian's comment about Eris in the 11th square the nodes, there's chaos that prevents long-term goals from being achieved. The two bodies on the North Node are in Capricorn, the sign of working for the long haul. Something that you really want – Venus on the North Node – being prevented from happening because of some external chaos.

When you were a little kid and were asked what you want to be when you grow up, did you have an idea and when do you think it developed? And it's okay if you say it was when you were 38 or 45 – that's okay.

Summer: I didn't know that as a young kid.

Tom: So mid-30s? Give me an idea.

Summer: It seemed like I didn't have time to go inward because I got married really young and had two kids, and was married for 27 years – and served. And cared and loved it. I was happy and enjoyed it all.

Tom: That's one of the things with Venus on the North Node: what do you want? And adding Ceres in there: what really feeds you? And you might sacrifice that because you have Pluto in the 4th and South Node in Cancer – for family. You probably have lives where you don't do what you want ever because of your commitments to family and you love it! But the Venus gets left out, what really lights you up.

Jillian: What about Persephone being there, too?

Tom: Good, thank you – Persephone is there, too. Abducting yourself into pleasure that nurtures your soul. [group laughs]

Summer: Oh, wow.

Michael: We do that – that's a good idea!

Tom: You can think about how different versions of you over time – at 10, 20, 30 years old – would answer this series of questions: "What do you want? What would make you happy? What do you need right now? Is there something you can imagine that's better that you're not quite sure how to do yet but you want?" That's part of the Persephone thing here because she is the puer, the maiden archetype. She doesn't know something and that's why she needs someone to come by and snatch her away into some new reality. She actually doesn't know how to grow up so she needs the Lord of the Underworld to teach her how to be a woman. So Persephone doesn't know it but now you're an adult and you can abduct yourself. [group laughs and claps] Thanks for pointing that out, by the way, Jillian, because I was really focused on those two other symbols.

Persephone, Ceres, Venus – these are feminine archetypes. We all know the truth that we have male and female within us but coming from patriarchy with a Cancerian South Node and Pluto in the house of identifying with history, the patriarchal imprint will be strong for you.

Jillian: Summer, do you feel pressure to stay young and not mature? Like you should stay a little girl or did you feel a lack of encouragement to grow up and be – stay cute and small?

Tom: And not be autonomous?

Summer: Without a doubt. That was kind of said without words in our family.

Jillian: To stay a little a girl because of all of this feminine.

Candace: Oh my god.

Jillian: Ceres is Persephone's mom. And this might come especially from women to stay small in the world.

Summer: Yep.

Tom: When you work these energies in Capricorn – it's the sign of the voice of authority. So if you work them, everybody else who's supposed to be Capricorn around you – traditional, stereotypical masculine: firm, clear, and in charge – might be threatened.

Summer: If I show up?

Tom: If you were to do these things. Venus in Capricorn: "This is what's important to me – bottom line, not budging." [group laughs] Planets in Capricorn take time to mature because we have to figure out how to grow up – this part of us. For you it's Venus and your value system had to grow up. Married for 27 years – how old were you when you got married?

Summer: 21.

Tom: And then the kids happened right away, right?

Summer: Two years.

Tom: You probably lived out a patriarchal marriage where the woman's values didn't get reflected in how the relationship worked.

Summer: Yes.

Tom: Venus on the North Node. How long did you know the man you married before marrying him?

Summer: A couple of years.

Tom: Were you involved for that long?

Summer: I had met him but no, we were not involved. But we lived together for a year before we got married.

Tom: What I want to know is when things went to the romantic/sexual/partner level, was that very quick?

Summer: Yes, actually.

Tom: Like quicker than anybody in your family was comfortable with? Like over the course of a few weeks suddenly it got real serious?

Summer: You know what? It did. He proposed to me and I didn't know and wanted to think about it, and he followed it up with, "I'm not going to ask you again." And I should have taken that there right then as a sign.

Jillian: That's pressure!

Candace: She was totally pressured.

Tom: That's an abduction – that's what I'm getting at. The sudden –

Summer: And I just kind of followed along. I still loved, and I was intrigued spiritually, being drawn into the church and all that stuff but now when I look at it, I was – I can see now how that was a good lesson for teaching me to value myself and what my needs are as opposed to others' needs.

Jillian: She said it was not only the man but the Christian church, too.

Summer: And his family and the whole thing.

Tom: That's what I wanted to get at, too. I was going to ask in what way was he Capricorn because you would have a Capricorn abductor. When you went into marriage as Persephone and you became queen of that Capricorn underworld – you became the queen. But it doesn't mean you felt honored but within that context you were respected and honored. I think you've learned it but I just want to touch on it to give you words for how to abduct yourself into what works. You had a chance to be abducted into something that worked because you got to flex that Cancerian South Node/Pluto-in-the-4th family muscle. And how fulfilling!

Summer: It was very purposeful.

Tom: You said it was being of service and that you loved it. So great. But now your choice comes in and has to be the bottom line – this Venus. What makes you feel nurtured, what makes you feel lit up and alive and loved and loving. It's not just about being of service.

This is a signature of somebody who has a best friend who says – and you guys were laughing earlier when I said something like this – "Why don't you ever do anything that you wanna do?" You might be habituated to think of responsibilities and kids and the friend says, "But your kids are in their 20s. Why are you waiting to enjoy something? They don't need you right now. Take a week off." But you're committed to the family vibe and to the stability, security, and the nest. This is a signature of somebody who chooses not to enjoy things because she feels needed.

Eventually all children grow up so then you have to make the decision to abduct yourself into enjoying life after that happens.

Summer: And that's literally what I did.

Tom: Was it hard?

Summer: It was hard in a lot of ways but it made it easy to fall into music. It provided an arena where there was already so much acceptance and so much individuality in the music world that I could just – it gave me a forum in which I could feel completely comfortable and just let go in my own little world while dancing. Where I could find that joy and that bliss and just let it out. So I guess I abducted myself!

Tom: Good. We all have to do that. Otherwise we're waiting for something interesting to happen.

Summer: It feels so safe that I could just stay there, you know? But I feel like there's something – maybe it's in my chart – but I feel like I came here for service, but maybe that's just because I'm so familiar with it that I feel standing on my own authority in some kind of way in my love – I feel like I'm somehow a part of the consciousness shift and that I came here to be a light in some way. There's a little but of fear sort of wrapped around it, too. I've found some of the dark spots – what if I stand out too much? What if I get snuffed because I'm standing in love and for the people waking up, and standing for the soul? Maybe there's a history of getting shut down for that.

Jillian: Sun-Mercury on her Midheaven opposite Pluto and Pluto as power and the fear of death. But your Sun is on the Midheaven – you're on stage and it's in the sign of Aquarius, which involves community and the New Age. So yeah – you're already doing it.

Tom: There's something in the past to be healed, and this is where I want to go. I want to move on to the South Node ruler, which is step 3. It's in Virgo in the 5th house. She's coming from Cancerian people in the 2nd house with this confusion about relationships and pleasure and allowing chaos to shift your goals – that's the context. She shows up as Virgo in the 5th house. Virgo is service-oriented. Now we have to tell this story specifically in terms of a Capricorn North Node with Venus on it because you're taught to show up with the spirit of service but you're never taught how to grow up. To become empowered to do something constructive that makes the kind of difference that you want to make. Meaning this North Node in Earth with Venus – your value system – as far away from your family system as possible. You're showing up with, "I want to do something!" And they're like, "You can be useful by doing the dishes." And you respond with, "Well, I see how that helps and I'll do that but I want to get to do something *really* important." And they're like, "Oh, yeah – totally. Would you go out and milk the goats?" [group laughs] And then 2 years later you're thinking, "Okay ... this is not changing" – right? You need to be abducted. It is into maturity but the kind of tension that comes from being a younger person in a family in patriarchal society the last 6,000 years ... if you're a boy, there are expectations that you grow up and do certain things and that can bring Venus on the North Node: "I didn't get to choose what I did – I didn't get to do what I felt was important." If you're a girl, even less.

There are these stories we have about being a boy in our history – "at least they got to do what they wanted." Well, if you're the 4th of 4 boys, maybe not. The oldest one decided to be a priest, the second one became a soldier, and the third one an attorney or banker. The three best jobs just got taken and you can't repeat one. So even though you're a boy and we might assume you had it easy, you had to go do something you didn't even want to do. You really wanted to be a soldier or a priest, maybe. What I'm getting at is that regardless of gender you haven't gotten to choose what you do. So you're showing up to be of service but in some ways don't ever feel empowered to do something that seems worthwhile to you. It can be a life of doing the dishes.

Bringing in the intimate relationship idea that goes with the 8th house: Ceres in the 7th and Venus-Persephone on the North Node. You have plenty of relationships but they don't fit what matters to you. And they don't feed your heart and soul. You might even be in relationships where you're being served in a Cancerian way, you know like I said to you about being best of service if you do the dishes, but you could also be the person essentially brainwashed into thinking that girls are best at doing dishes and milking the goats.

Summer: And I choose to do that.

Tom: Right, and then you're a man or a woman and you're clear that this is how we do things, how we will teach our daughters to be. From all these different angles, it's shown up for you that what *really* matters to you might not be achievable. Not knowing what you want to do is an adaptation to try to save you pain later because you won't get to do it. [group "ohs"] Get it? It's an adaptation: "I'm not going to get do it anyway so why should I bother identifying it?"

Candace: Whoa!

Summer: Because it's so far away.

Tom: It's as far away from the family system, the conditioning, the families of origin as possible. It's as far away from the comfort zone as possible.

Candace: But the abduction into maturity is what she gets to choose to do now?

Tom: If she believes she has the right and is the right kind of adult. I want to say this next bit and then give her an idea on the strata to work on the archaeological dig.

Summer: I'm still writing that – that last part was?

Tom: If you believe that you're the right kind of adult, and that's where I want to go next to explain what that means.

Candace: Wow.

Anne: What you believe is what you get.

Tom: That's right. A side note here. With a body on the North Node we tend to fall in three camps. We didn't get to have it – that's the bottom line. It wasn't available to us, nobody taught us how to do it, we didn't get to have it – we felt blocked from it. Sometimes people will keep it from us or keep us from it. One is: *I will have that no matter what – I'm determined because I didn't get to have it before.* There's a minority there. The second one is also a minority: *Oh, I don't get to have that. I don't deserve that. Other people get to have that but not me.* The third one, which is the majority is people vacillating between those two constantly. [group laughs] Vacillating or oscillating – going back and forth: *I really, really want this! I'm determined to have it! But gosh, I feel so disempowered, I'm not going to bother.* Two years later: *I have to have it! Oh, no, murmur murmur.* Or: *I feel sorry for myself. Don't feel sorry! I deserve that.* Up and down with it. That's what most of us do when we have something conjunct the North Node. It could be that you have 5 years or a decade or two of total empowerment or disempowerment with it but usually there is a lot of back and forth because you are confronting your belief – the karma – that you don't get to have it and then you get to respond to that belief. *Really?! Dammit, I want it! Don't tell me what I can't do.*

What I want to tell you fits with this. Feeling empowered to get really good at something, that you have the time and space emotionally and physically – real world-wise – to work on something and it's Venus. So there's an art in there. In some lives you're longing to do art – could be dancing or anything else creative – but to do the creative thing that just isn't available but longing to do it.

The 8th-house intimacy side of this configuration is in choosing relationships. This is a marker of marrying because you're supposed to marry or marrying the people you marry because you're supposed to. Or having things set up for you. There's a Cancerian value system in play in your relationships and because of the heavy emphasis on family you'll sacrifice the fire of getting lit up emotionally – all the rooms in your house having the doors fly open erotically when you encounter somebody. Like every door flies open within you – every chakra, all corners of your heart. That kind of Venus in the 8th house that is not available to you. So having relationships chosen for you or choosing because of a value system that isn't yours.

Summer: [laughs] That's what I did!

Tom: I could tell from the conversation earlier.

Summer: What's interesting is that when I'm in my own world I'm not dancing to attract other people. I'm really doing my own healing work for myself and for all the people that I love and the Earth. But I feel like my Venus is too wide open, especially when I'm in the dancing zone, I guess, because I just let myself go.

Tom: Because you do attract people?

Summer: I feel like I'm maybe possibly too shiny, too open, and it threatens others.

Tom: Okay, so this is good! How other people respond to you has nothing to do with you – a basic truth. So please shine. In every way you can. Sometimes you'll get tired and you'll pull back from an edge. Some weeks you'll choose not to shine at all. But for you to open up is actually giving a gift of Venus to others. Because this setup says that you need to learn to embody Venus. It's in the 8th house and you might inspire people. They might have doors in their house fly open just watching you and they know –

Summer: They do. People just come up and hug me and they're teary-eyed.

Tom: Exactly! So that's your Venus, and when you do it you do Ceres at the same time so it has a nurturing quality, a loving quality to it. All those people for you are teachers to hold space for you. They are saying, "Please keep doing this – you're really having a wonderful effect."

Jillian: And alongside that, the Moon is in the 5th house. You need to play and dance and you do it in service to others by doing that – it's Virgo. When you said it was Venus I felt more of the Moon in Virgo – what naturally makes you happy, where you gravitate, and dancing does that.

Glenna: You're shining your inner world out because it's in the 5th house and the beauty of it is coming out.

Tom: Plus, you get to upgrade the notion of what service is or should be.

Jillian: Right. You just being happy and dancing is serving others. How about that? No dishes involved. [group laughs]

Tom: But art in this karmic story has not been valued, so if she shows up and wants to be of service and somebody says, "Go milk the goats," she might say, "Well, that fits so I'll go do that."

Jillian: "Well, I'll dance for you." [group laughs]

Annette: Exactly.

Tom: People who get really focused on service need to hear this. I get told this because I get into this place of doing all this kind of work and I'm not going to write the satire that I want to write. And people ask me what am I talking about because laughter heals. I often feel like I have to do this and they say, "No, please!" It's conflict. Because what is healing? We've been conditioned by what healing is to look like. And then especially with a Virgo Moon, feeling useful whatever you choose to do. It's always a natural tension of if you choose something pleasurable for you, can you really believe that that's actually useful for others?

Summer: Somehow I have arranged it in my dancing that I can just feel utter love for all and that it's still being useful because I know – I feel that love going out. I send it.

Tom: That's the empowered way of doing it.

Anne: When you're feeding yourself, you're feeding others also.

Summer: Absolutely.

Annette: It goes back to those many past lives that you've lived – dance used to have an intention in many times and places. The Indians do a dance for rain. There are lots of different dances. So when you're out there doing your dance, how much of you from another time is present?

Tom: Can I ask you a question? When you first brought up that people do respond they come up to you and hug you, you had that sudden rush of emotion as you talked. Can you describe that a little? I want to know what is going on with that intense emotion that accompanies their reaction.

Summer: It amazes me to see the invisible world show up and for people to see in the physical the effect of the love, intention, and togetherness, and spirit. Maybe it's part of me that I have a hard time accepting that I'm the vessel for this.

Tom: That's what I wanted to get at. The more peace you can make with that and accepting their love that you are inspiring. And letting them hold you.

Summer: When I'm with them I don't even have to cry and I'm in that zone. I'm not in the kind of space I'm in right now. [group laughs]

Tom: Good. So drink it in when they bring it to you. They're loving you because you're loving everybody. Thank you for all of that.

Then the 4th step – we've been talking about the 8th-house North Node because of the Venus. So the 4th step of the process: what does she not really know about as a soul?

What is the soul needing to learn as her? We talked about the choice and the nurturing. What I want to talk about are all the doors in the house that is you flung open in response to somebody. The 8th house is not just where we couple with people or where we merge resources but it's where we open ourselves. But if you don't feel chemistry you can't open. I just want to point out this side of the Venus on this North Node in the 8th, keeping an eye on and radar attuned to what you are attracted to and why. Part of you might be willing to partition different kinds of attraction. We could make a list of what kinds of things you find attractive but that list might be informed by 2nd-house conditioning regarding practicality but we're talking about the importance of chemistry and seeing stars – that image of all the doors in the house that is you flung open, that's really where I want to keep coming back to. I've said it 4 times or so. I've never had that image before but I get it when I think about you and where you're coming from with that karmic history. It's about every portion of you being addressed. What I want to say is that it serves you well by not settling for anything less. If you marry someone that you're not fully attracted to and you end up giving that person 15 children, that affects how you deal with attraction in other lives. And this is in Capricorn so it might happen slowly over time. It might not be as sparky and speedy as it might be with this setup in Aries, for example, but for you to feel all levels of you engaged – all of the levels in your house are occupied, all the doors are open, and the lights are on in every room – that's an even better extension of it. The completeness of experience in the 8th house where all parts of you are engaged – that's been left out. That's a good barometer now, not to settle for less ever – paralleling how you experience the dancing: *open*. So relationships need to do that to you, too, and there's power in choice. With Venus on the Capricorn North Node in the 8th, in various lives you haven't always been choosing.

Summer: It's all about choice and I feel like that's what my life has been about.

Tom: And saying "yes, please" to what works and "no thanks" to what doesn't work, like we were talking about with Michael learning to say yes and no – same thing.

Jillian: After Tom asked you what happens for you when people come up to hug you when you're dancing, you said that the invisible can be visible, that this love – which is Venus – in the 8th house of mystical communion and Venus in Capricorn – love made manifest. Making something solid, with structure.

Annette: Sometimes showing up with intimacy in our society is a really scary thing to do. And if you're pure love and pure intimate and you're dancing, it can put people in touch with all kinds of feelings – it's a visual extension and physical extension of what you feel in your heart.

Tom: Great, thank you.

About the Author

Tom Jacobs is an Evolutionary Astrologer, Medium, and Channel. A graduate of Evolutionary Astrologer Steven Forrest's Apprenticeship Program, he has a global practice of readings and coaching to help people understand what they came to Earth to do and supporting them in making it happen. Tom is the author or channel of twelve books on astrology, mythology, and spirituality and original astrological natal reports on Lilith and the shifts happening now that culminate in 2012. He offers a groundbreaking audio course on Chiron based on channelings from Ascended Master Djehuty, "Chiron, 2012, and the Aquarian Age: The Key and How to Use It."

Contact Tom Jacobs via http://tdjacobs.com.

Made in the USA
Middletown, DE
22 November 2022